THE TIME IS NOW

I0626978

Author's Notes

May we remember the names of those who overcame despite the circumstances they couldn't control, the chaos and the challenges that were around them, and the spoken and unspoken battles that lived inside of them. Say their names.

We know that overcoming, being victorious, and triumphant is our portion because there were heroes who not only lived but chose to be ALIVE despite those circumstances.

To the late
Mazell Mae Strayhorn,
Maragret Lee Strayhorn
and Vicky Louise Strayhorn.

PART ONE:
The journey to the Breakthrough and Transition

First Love

Inherited Habits and The Tasmanian Devil

The Black Sheep and Moses

Counterfeits, Placeholders, Shapeshifters and Tears

To The Breaking Then Transition

PART TWO:
The Journey to the Promise

The Predator

The Remnant

Unlearning, Relearning and Esther

The Promise Part 1

THE TIME IS NOW

PART ONE :
THE JOURNEY TO THE
BREAKTHROUGH AND
TRANSITION

"I remember when I was young

And your voice shouting loud my name

And since that moment

I haven't heard it quite that way

Well, now that I'm older

Could you say it again?

I remember when I was afraid

And, oh, the hand I felt lead the way

And for the first time in my life, I felt safe

Well, God, now that I'm older

Would you lead me again?

Oh, take me back, back

All the way back

Oh, take me back to my first love."

FIRST LOVE

Times were a little different when I was growing up. In a city up north, life was a little bit simpler. Technology didn't control the mind and actions of people. If you didn't want to hear or see what was going on in the world, you could simply turn off your television.

These were the days when you knew the people in your neighborhood; when you could sit on your porch and greet everyone by name as they passed by.

During these times, most of the population was the working class. You would work two to three jobs to make ends meet for your family and as you and your spouse were at work, the kids would be at "Big Momma's house".

The country was in a war in the Middle East. The culture was infused with gangsta rap, and it greatly influenced how most people talked, dressed, and lived. Some called these people "thugs" but to many of us, these people were influencers and advocates for the black and brown culture. This culture was being expressed in many ways like in fashion, music, poetry, television shows, and food. Most say these were the best years of our lives. Television had many sitcoms and movies on black and brown families, love, and prosperity. These were the times when you were transitioning from playing music on cassette tapes to CD players. When you couldn't be on the house phone and the internet at the same time. Where your house phone had a cord and adults had pagers. Those were the days when you would go to church every Sunday with your grandmother. Prayer, church, and Jesus weren't a choice or anything to be questioned.

The hot comb would be ready on Saturday so you would look presentable on Sunday. Those were the days when the stench of your grandfather's shaving cream would leave a horrible smell in the whole house; when the library was just down the street, and it was your favorite safe place. During winter, you would put on a whole snowsuit because the snow would come up to your knees. You could walk to school and back and not fear for your life; where the music that your mother or grandmother played in the house on Saturday mornings would let you know that it was time to clean. The same music was played so much that it stained your memory, so you could never forget the sound of artists like The Stylistics singing...

"You're alone all time

Does it ever puzzle you, have you asked why?

You seem to fall in love, out again

Do you ever really love or just pretend

Why fool yourself

Don't be afraid to help yourself

It's never too late, too late to

Stop, look

Listen to your heart, hear what it's saying

Stop, look

Listen to your heart, hear what it's saying

Love, love, love"

or old Gospel's artists like The Williams Brothers
singing...

"And he said, "On the street's day and night

That's my life, that's my home

Ain't got nowhere else I could go

So I just walk the streets

Telling the people about Jesus

From corner to corner, from door to door.

But they all make fun of me and say...

I'm just a nobody trying to tell everybody

About somebody, who can save anybody

I'm just a nobody trying to tell everybody

About somebody, who can save anybody"

These were also during the times when going through hard times was just that. You went through it and never talked about it, especially in the black community. In fact, during these times, no one talked about their problems. Because they didn't have the proper resources and distrusted clinicians (who at the time didn't look like them or understand them), they would eventually have a mental breakdown or experience some kind of trauma that would change their lives forever. So black people would suppress, go to work, and "move on" as their hearts grew cold over time, and as cycles of trauma and dysfunction ravaged through families, generation after generation. Everyone knew how to manage, cover, cope and hide these behaviors to fit the social norm and if you couldn't, a psychiatric hospital is where you were taken and given a green wristband to let you and others know that you were mentally ill.

I never understood these things growing up, but for some reason, it really frustrated me. But, as Mamo would say "that's just how things were, baby."

For me? It never failed that around the end of each day, I would be the only one who always found myself sitting on the floor between the door and the closet of the room I shared with my mom, waiting to get in trouble for having another one of my blow-ups. I would sit there anxiously waiting on what was going to happen next. Would I get a whooping, get yelled at, a talk, or all three? Either way, it wouldn't be anything new for me. Every time my sisters and I were around each other long enough, one of them would always make me mad by playing around too much when I didn't want to be bothered or by not giving me what I wanted when I wanted it. I was the baby of three girls, and I was cute if I do say so myself. How could I not become spoiled rotten?

Mom allowed my sisters and me to either play in my sisters' room, the living room or downstairs when Mamo and Papo were at work. No matter the place, I would eventually get in trouble. I didn't know why. I just knew that most of the time I was angry, and when I wasn't angry, I was extremely on edge so it wouldn't take much to get me to have one of my temper tantrums and end up here: in our room, sitting on the floor in between the door and the closet, waiting to get in trouble for having one of my blow-ups.

My mother came into the room, fed up and sick and tired of me as usual. She asked with no kind of enthusiasm, "Kayla, did you hit both of your sisters when it was their turn to play the game and not yours?"

"No," I said.

"No, what?" She spoke.

"No ma'am" I replied.

She knew I was lying. She grabbed me by the hand, took me to my sisters' room, and forced me to apologize.

"Kayla! Say sorry, right now!" She demanded. Embarrassed and angry, I rolled my eyes and still apologized. I did whatever I had to do to get out of whatever trouble I was in, as soon as possible, so I could play again.

After all of that was said and done, I still had to stay in my room until my mother said I could leave the room. She never came back that day to release me though.

I started to get mad all over again because I was left there with my thoughts and emotions that I couldn't control. When I was playing and doing other things, I could stop thinking about stuff, but when I wasn't, I had to face the thoughts. I didn't want to. So, I began to kick the door and make myself cry so I wouldn't have to think.

Each kick on the door got louder and louder. I hoped my little foot would at least break something or my cry would make my mother sad enough to come in and hug me, or even better let me out of the room. I began to get exhausted from all the energy I was putting in and could no longer fight the thoughts.

"Why did the boy, who was supposed to be my cousin, touch me?" I thought.

 I knew it was bad, but now I couldn't control my feelings and thoughts. I just wanted them to stop.

 "Am I supposed to tell someone when something like that happens?" the thoughts continued.

I shook the thoughts off and tucked that experience in the back of my head and tried to forget about it.

Nighttime quickly came and like all the other nights, my anger quickly turned to fear as the time came to go to bed.

The same closet I would sit by, hide and play in or wait by whenever I got in trouble would be the same closet, I would be afraid of when the nighttime came.

Mommy and I shared a room together while my two sisters shared a room down the hall and Mamo and Papo had the basement. I hated nighttime and I hated the basement. Don't let it be nighttime and I must go to the basement for anything. Whatever was left downstairs will be there until the next day when I went downstairs with someone.

The dark scared me so much, just like any little 6-year-old girl. Because of my fear of the dark, I would have nightmares and pee in bed most nights. Mommy would just say that I was a wild sleeper. She would tell me that I would kick her, hit her, or end up cuddling very close to her when I slept. Most nights were bad. I would wake up out of my dreams terrified and crying or just wake up and go back to sleep. I never really remembered what happened. I just knew I would be afraid by the time I fell asleep and afraid when I woke up out of my dreams. Just like my thoughts, I couldn't control them or how they would make me feel.

The morning came quickly, and I had to hurry and get ready before I missed the school bus. Right before I walked out the door, I glanced at the calendar to see how close my birthday was. From the looks of it, something needed to start changing in my behavior so I could get exactly what I wanted and so mom wouldn't cancel my bowling party. I had one month until my birthday and the party, so I knew I had to start getting to work. I started waking up without any complaints. I went from arguing with my sisters and fighting with them to sharing and being nice. I would complain in private before and after doing my chores and I started trying to do better in school.

School wasn't my favorite place to be either and it was hard for me. I was in first grade at the time and my teacher was Mrs. Wright. My sisters and I all had her as our first-grade teacher, and she loved us. If I could, I would have invited her to my birthday party too, but mommy said I could only invite 5 of my friends from my class.

I started to realize that I was not only different at home, but I was also different at school too. I couldn't get along with anyone at school except my sisters. They were the only ones who understood me. No one really liked me in Mrs. Wright's class except a few kids and I never understood why. I tried to always be nice, but it never worked out the way I planned. I chose to invite 5 kids from my class who I really wanted to like me. I was tired of being the odd one out and I really wanted friends.

I made the decision to not only change my behavior and be good at home but to also try to be better in school and try even harder to have friends.

Weeks passed and my behavior progressed. It was one week until my birthday party and my mission every day, as I counted down, was to do everything I said I was going to do, no matter how hard it was or how tired I got.

Yes, I wanted to be good at school, at home, and get better at making friends so I could not only have my birthday party and have kids from my school there celebrating with me, but I also wanted my wish to come true. You see, for the last two years in a row, I had wished for the same thing for my birthday every time I blew out the candles after everyone had sung the birthday song to me. I wished that my father's face would be staring back at me as I opened my eyes after blowing out the candles on my cake.

My dad wasn't in my life much and he and mom never married. I was the product of a relationship that was already ending. He wasn't there when I was born. His name wasn't on my birth certificate, and I didn't have his last name. I was called two things, the "chaos baby" and the "surprise baby". I was called the "chaos baby" because I was conceived during the time when my mother and father argued and fought the most. Some say that was probably the reason for my bad behavior. Along with being called the "chaos baby", I was also the "surprise baby" because after my mother had my sisters Briana and Marchea, everyone thought she was done having children. No one knew she was pregnant with me until her due date. My mother had always said, "you were a surprise to everyone else, but not to me." She did say, however, that what surprised her was my gender. She had already had two girls at that point, and she had no

doubt that I would be her last and that I would be a

boy. Kaleb was the chosen name until 2:44 am, on

May 21st when I was born, and the name quickly

changed from Kaleb to Kayla.

My father visited a few times not too long after my

mother gave birth to me, but that's all they were...

just visits.

It had been almost two years since I had seen my father. I was turning 8 and I was tired of the visits. I wanted my daddy. I didn't know what had happened before I was born but all I wanted was my mother and father to work things out, so we could be like the families I saw on TV like on Good Times, Family Matters, and The Cosby Show. All had mothers and fathers. All had what I so desperately wanted: a normal life and a normal family.

All I wanted for my birthday that year was for my father to at least come to my birthday party, make up for the time that had passed, and show the kids from school that I was normal. That is all I ever really wanted, and I just knew that that year would be the year something would change!

Saturday came quickly and I didn't need an alarm to wake me up on this day! It was still very early, and the party didn't start until 1:30 pm. That didn't matter much though, because we had so much left to do. First things first, everyone in the house had to get ready and pack up the party decorations, and drinks and head over to Larosa's to pick up the pizzas before hurrying to the bowling sly to decorate and set up. Then Mommy and Mamo were going to pick up my cake once Uncle Toby got there to keep an eye on us.

We arrived at the bowling alley and unloaded the car.

"Don't get your hopes up, okay?" Mommy said.

"For the kids from school to come?" I asked, confused.

"No, for your daddy." She answered.

"Yes ma'am," I said back to her.

I still believed in my heart that my Daddy was

coming, and nothing was going to change that. I

ignored her and moved on.

We got to work right away. Decorations were being

set and my family and I easily got into the party spirit.

Uncle Toby arrived and Mamo and Mommy headed

over to get the cake. The kids started to show up and

as the first round of bowling began, I looked around

and noticed that my father hadn't arrived yet.

Princeton Bowl was one of my favorite places to go to as a kid and it became the spot for every birthday, family outing, and surprise outing if we all were good. I always enjoyed bowling but as you walked into the bowling alley, down the hall on the left from the front desk, there was an opening into an arcade where I always loved to play. Once my mother and Mamo came back with the cake, three of the kids I invited and so desperately wanted to be friends with, came. Asia, Caleb, and Azmara came ready to have fun and we all became friends in the arcade, playing games that made all of us happy. Then, we decided to bowl! Azmara and Caleb versus Asia and me. I never knew how to bowl correctly but it didn't matter at this point because we were having so much fun. It seemed like Caleb and Azmara were going to win at first, but they didn't. We won! I was so happy and was having so much fun with my friends, cousins, and sisters that I completely forgot about the time. My mom called us when it was time to cut the cake and reminded us that the party would soon be over.

But as I started calming down from the sugar rush from the candy and fun from the games, I once again noticed my father's absence. I was so disappointed, but I chose to put it in the back of my head, blow out the candles on the cake, act like nothing happened, and enjoy the rest of my birthday party with the people who showed up.

After the party, we all went home. To everyone else, it was a normal Saturday but not for me. When the rest of my family got home, they watched TV downstairs. Me? I sat there alone in my room, body tensed and head thumping trying to figure out "why?"

It's the same question I had asked myself ever since I noticed that my life was different. My family was different. I was different. I wanted what everyone else seemed to have.

"Why does everyone around me have everything I ever wanted and desired but me?"

I was trapped in my own head, by my own thoughts like a prisoner in a cell with the door wide open. To someone looking from the outside in, my freedom was right in front of me.

"But she could easily just stop thinking about it if she wanted to," they would say.

But I knew that a simple escape wouldn't resolve my issue. My question would still be left unanswered, and I would only be temporarily relieved. My mind would eventually go back to the same question. I needed to know the reason why! Then and only then, would my problem be truly resolved.

I couldn't take it anymore. I got up and walked out of the room, searching for my mother.

"Mommy!" I yelled.

"What girl?!" Mom responded from the bathroom across the hall.

I followed my mother's voice straight into the bathroom. I didn't knock nor ask to come in. I just walked right in.

"What girl?!" My mother asked again.

I stared at my little black face in the mirror.

"Maybe I'm the problem," I thought.

"Girl! If you don't answer me!" My mother demanded.

My mother was taking another box of Kleenex out of the cabinet in the bathroom.

"Why isn't daddy ever here?" I finally gathered up the courage to ask.

It was like I had finally exploded and could no longer contain myself.

"At school, when we have 'breakfast with dad', instead of daddy showing up, you show up... When I call, he never answers? When he does answer and I want to see him, he never shows up. Like today, he didn't show up and he didn't even call. He's never here. Why is he not here?!"

Silence consumed the bathroom for what seemed to be forever as my mother's countenance changed from annoyance to hopelessness and then sadness. As I looked into my mother's beautiful brown eyes, it was as if I could see an internal struggle.

She finally mustered up the courage and said "I don't know Kayla. I told you not to get your hopes up" she answered with disappointment.

Pushing away from the sadness, my mom's face lit up with a big smile.

"But I know someone who can be your father! But baby, you must let Him into your heart," My mother grinned as she took my little brown face into both hands.

Looking confused, I answered, "how do I do that Mommy?"

"You start by praying, but everything else? You must figure it out on your own."

I went back into my room, but this time I was a little more hopeful and excited. I got on my knees like I had seen my mama do many times and just started talking to this person that was supposedly going to solve the very problem I had. I wasn't sure how that was going to happen, but you can say, I stepped out on faith.

"God, I don't know what I'm doing or how to do this, but I want you here! They say a girl's first love is her father. I want that love! I'm mad all the time, I don't know how to calm down, I don't know what to do about being touched by my cousin. I always get in trouble. I am so different!"

"God, I just want my daddy. My mommy said you could help me get my daddy… could you do that for me, please? I want a daddy so bad; I'll do anything. I promise I'll do anything for that. I'm choosing to trust you. Please, God, I hope you can hear me."

"Train up a child in the way he should go,
And when he is old, he will not depart from it."
Proverbs 22:6

INHERITED HABITS AND THE TASMANIAN DEVIL

I came from a big family, but my family was very different from the typical two-parent household with children and a dog. I just didn't have that type of family. I lived with three generations of women, my two sisters, and my grandfather. Papo was a countryman who always worked two jobs and always had two or more cars. Mamo, his wife, was my grandmother. She was a short, thick, and lighter-skinned woman who always reminded me of a young Etta James. Though she couldn't sing, she would always say "Baby, if I had a voice, I would be bad!" I would say Mamo was my first teacher of many things. She taught me how to be bold, stern, and soft as a woman, but she wasn't the best at showing or expressing more vulnerable emotions. She saw them as weaknesses. She was bold and strong most of the time and when she got angry, she would explode. My mother was the opposite. Mommy was a little taller. She had a beautiful, darker skin complexion. She was slim, thick, and a lot more soft-spoken. My mother didn't deal with conflict very well. She was more submissive in a way. She was also known to be stuck, not only mentally but physically as well. Not only was my mother more unassertive but she didn't show much emotion either. I had only seen my mother cry twice before this time: one time in church but she hurried and ran to the bathroom so we couldn't see and one cold winter day when my mother, sisters and I were having a snowball fight and my sister Marchea hit her in the face by accident.

When my father and mother ended their relationship, before she got pregnant with me, she moved in with our grandparents. My mother was forced to be a single mother of three children at a young age, gave up her dreams and goals, put her whole entire life on hold to provide for us, and possibly many more things that she had never expressed to anyone. I didn't know then that all these experiences could result in someone having depression. I also didn't know that her cycles of feeling deep sadness, resulting in isolation and feelings of hopelessness, were symptoms of depression and that they could hold someone captive like that, let alone my own mother.

Lastly, there was my great-grandmother, Little Mama. Little Mama was a sweet, smaller-built, light skin woman. Like my mother, she was also soft-spoken. Just in case you couldn't tell by my behavior, I didn't want to be soft-spoken, so I gravitated towards my grandmother's personality the most. I saw that quality in my mother and great-grandmother, and I thought they were weak because of it. I didn't want to be weak. I wanted to be a fighter, strong, and tough, even though I didn't need to be back then because I was a child. But eventually, I wouldn't have a choice.

I was more expressive and energetic than both of my older sisters. Briana was yellow and skinny and looked just like our Daddy. Marchea was tall like our daddy but had beautiful dark skin and looked just like our mother. Both were spitting images of our parents. As for me, I was a mixture of both. My skin tone was in between my mother and father, and I was told that I had the worst parts of both. My mother would say that my anger and mischievous behavior came from my father, but other family members would say that my sensitivity came from my mother because I cried so much.

Nonetheless, I was never taught how to deal with either side. Mommy would tell me to stop crying because "big girls don't cry "so I never learned how to express how I felt in any other way other than in anger or in tears. No one knew how much I was storing and stuffing away. But when Sunday came, everything was different. We all went to church on Sundays except for Papo. That was our safe place.

During that point in time, church was the center of many families and the lives of many people. I grew up during a time when going to church was not a negotiation. You would go with either your parents or grandparents. This was also the place where most black people found relief, peace, and hope. At this specific point in my life and for my family, it was a huge part of our lives and everything about church gave us hope.

It was Sunday, around 7:30 am and it was time to get ready for church. It was just a little after the sun rose, when my alarm in human form, Mamo, opened my bedroom door, telling me to wake up. This Sunday started off a little differently than usual. Normally my mom would have our food ready so we could eat in the car on the way to church. Everyone would be in a hurry and in a rush to get dressed so they could get there on time because the church was on the other side of town. The sound of Marvin Sapp singing would fill the rooms of the entire house:

"Never would have made it

Never would have made it, without you

I would have lost it all."

or

Kirk Franklin and Family singing

"I never knew

I could be so happy

I never knew

I'd be so secure

Because of your love

Life has brand new meaning

It's gonna be a brighter day, brighter day."

But this Sunday was different. No music was playing throughout the house and the morning went slow. My sisters and I ate at the house and Mamo and Little Mama weren't stressed about getting to church on time. Everyone got dressed slowly, loaded up the car, and went on to church. When we arrived, the Reverend hadn't started preaching yet but for some reason the atmosphere was different. The choir was up singing, and it seemed like they were just about done. The whole congregation was still standing as the usher directed us into the sanctuary. Fans were still fanning, tears still flowing, and eyes were still closed. I began to look all around the church and suddenly someone in the choir started singing a song everyone knew...

"Yesterday is gone

And tomorrow is new

Everything is gone undone

Now it's time for you to

Look forward to a brighter day

And a great expected end

It's a new day and a new beginning

It's a new day and a new beginning."

As I looked across the church, I noticed that everything had begun to slow down, and everything seemed to be moving in slow motion. Some people were screaming and crying while others had their hands raised up with tears rolling down their faces. It seemed like everyone in the church was in one accord singing this song with so much sincerity and passion. I was confused and eager at the same time. I began to feel this wind in the atmosphere that captivated my whole body. I felt a sense of wholeness and completeness on the inside of me that I couldn't explain. The voices in the church began to get louder as they sang the next part of the song repeatedly.

"My future, my blessing, my promise, my reward starts all over again."

"Mommy, what are they doing?" I asked my mother in a whisper, trying not to disrupt.

"This is devotion. They are worshiping... expressing themselves to God," she answered.

Each time this last part was sung, it seemed like the entire church went from complete surrender to hope. Everyone began to smile, dance, and jump as if something was on the way to them. I still didn't understand but I prayed.

"God, I don't understand what is going on here, but I want what they got. I want to be able to express myself in this way, God. I don't want to be angry anymore. Amen."

"Stand even when nights seem cold and

Stand when you can't feel your soul and

Stand when your dark past won't seem to go away

(Help me say) You can Stand

God is right by your side and

He will make everything alright

So if you can lift your hands

There's a plan and just Stand

If I cry it's alright

Cause it may be just what I need (hum)

Cause everybody hurts sometimes and

Every heart needs relief

Still I know where to go

To the one who understands

So no matter what tomorrow may bring

Still I Stand"

THE BLACK SHEEP AND MOSES

I had problems at home, but school was a whole different ball game. School had always been difficult for me, but it got worse as I got older.

"Angel's east! Angels' west, north, and south! Do your best to guard and watch us while we rest. Amen! Take ya time and do your best and you'll achieve success! 1, 2, 3, don't let the Devil win or take you out of character! "

Every single day before my sisters and I got on the bus, my mother would stop all three of us before we got out the door. We would eat breakfast, pray and finish off by saying what I considered to be our war cry. My family's house was close to our school as I got into the 4th grade. Every day when it was time to go to school, I would get strength for the day from my mother and my sisters. We would stand in front of the door, pray, cover each other, and say our war cry. But once I got on that bus and arrived at school, it was like stepping into hell itself. I would lose all my strength.

Mental disorders and self-hate were birthed in these educational institutions. It was like I had to cry out to God all over again once my bus arrived. Nothing much had changed from my experiences in first grade to now. The few friends I had made at my 8th birthday party either moved away or acted like they didn't know me when I saw them every day.

"Is this what happens when you grow up?" I thought.

School was still challenging because I was socially awkward and still didn't know how to make friends and learning had always been difficult for me. I could never focus on the task at hand. So many different things impacted my ability to learn effectively. I didn't know how to process the things I had experienced at home, my father's absence, my home dynamic, and last but certainly not least, Tasha Wilson.

Tasha Wilson was the girl who hated me and bullied me. Tasha and her friends never let the day go by without giving me some type of trouble. She was the one I hoped and prayed would miss school so I could have some peace. The crazy thing was that she didn't bully anyone else but me. Everything was usually fine during the day while we were in class, but when it was time for lunch and recess, that's when I needed those prayers to work the most. Teachers believed this was a great space for children to get fresh air and play, but that time of the day was the devil's playground for me.

This was the point in my life where I developed my problem-solving skills. I tried to avoid Tasha during recess at any cost. My school's playground was huge, and we had an overhang. Tasha and her friends never went under there so that's where I would hide until they found me one day.

The sun was out beaming and when I saw Tasha and her crew coming towards me, laughing as if they knew something I didn't, my heart dropped, and I froze.

"Were you talking about me?" She asked aggressively.

"Talking about you?" I responded.

Clearly, she was lying. She just wanted to hurt me. I didn't have any friends currently either. She slapped me in the face and pushed me to the ground. Everyone began to scream and laugh as I feared for my life.

A teacher came under the overhang and blew the whistle for us to line up. It was like God saw me and rescued me right in time. I went on with my day, acting like it never happened. I was too embarrassed to admit what had happened, so I didn't say anything. I locked it away in the back of my mind and threw away the key.
I knew I couldn't cry because "big girls don't cry!" I said to myself. I knew if I had said something to a teacher, nothing would have happened, and I would have been attacked again for being a snitch.

I tried to do what my mother taught me in the bathroom, which was to pray. So I did just that.

I found peace in praying to God by myself when I felt scared, embarrassed, and worried. It became such a routine every day in school that I would bring my CD player with me. I would play music on the bus to and from school and I would sneak my CD player into the lunchroom, which was right before recess, where I knew I would be bullied by Tasha and her crew. I decided to pray and listen to a specific song on the CD player which became like therapy to me. Listening to the song and being in prayer at lunch gave me the strength to conquer the 30 minutes outside with Tasha, her crew, and whatever else came my way. If things were harder than usual, I would go to the bathroom to cry and pray. I would sometimes sneak my CD player with me and listen to that song.

It taught me to stand in the midst of it all and be bold. It taught me not to be consumed by the fire around me.

Even though I had my family and my sisters, building this relationship with God helped me to not feel so alone. I didn't feel so much like the black sheep anymore. I felt like God was easy to find every time I sought Him out.

One night, I feared going to sleep and I decided to pray like I did in school when things affected me. After I prayed, I went to sleep.

This night, God showed me Moses in a dream. He was living in one land, left it, and came back for the Israelites in that same land. He delivered the Israelites out of the land they were in and led them into a promised land.

After that, God spoke to me in that dream and said that I would be doing the same thing Moses did. I woke up confused and didn't know who to talk to about it, so I locked it away in my head, along with the things I had experienced at home and the attacks from Tasha and her friends and moved on.

I tried to use the only two tools I felt like I had. I always tried to pray but when the bullying in school got worse, I would worship. But at some point, I felt like God was ignoring me and my prayers weren't doing anything anymore. Nothing was changing. I began to get frustrated because I already felt alone at home, alone at school, and now alone in my relationship with God.
I felt like my mother lied to me and now on top of being sexually abused by a family member, having so much anger, being bullied for being different, I was now starting to feel hopeless.

It had been a couple of years since I had heard from or seen my father and it affected how I behaved. I tried praying my anger away because things had gotten worse. I was getting in trouble in school just as much as I was getting in trouble at home and now, they were talking about the possibility of holding me back a grade.

When I heard the news, I sat in my room and wondered if I was really doing enough. I didn't think I was, so I got some pieces of paper to write on. On one piece of paper, I wrote "anger issues". On another, I wrote "daddy". I wrote "family" on the third one, and then "school" on the last one. On each paper, I wrote a prayer to God about each topic. I folded them up, stood up on my bed, and put them all on the ceiling fan. I felt like maybe I was too short to reach God. The ceiling fan was the highest place I could reach so I figured that it was high enough for my prayers to reach Him. I just wanted God to hear me and change my situation.

I felt so alone until I met him.

He was the first boy who made me cry and introduced me to depression. I met him in my class in middle school. We had first talked when Tasha was still bullying me. He was a tall, light-skinned boy with beautiful brown eyes, and he had always been nice to me. With him, I didn't feel alone, and I could survive the day, even when I was being bullied. I started noticing that liking him distracted me from all the things that I didn't know how to process and gave me relief, which was the very thing I wanted God to give me.

One day, I decided to be brave and tell him how I felt. I told him I liked him, hoping he liked me back so he could be my very first boyfriend, and guess what? He did like me back! I was so excited and happy! Everything that was wrong was turning right because I was finally with someone who made me feel seen and important. Receiving affection and attention, especially from a man, was so different but I fell in love with that feeling.

From that day on, I was in the clouds. He became my first thought in the morning and my last one at night. Every day was amazing because I got to see him and when we both got home from school in the evening, we would get on the phone and talk all night until we fell asleep. We would wake up and do it all over again. The feeling that I had, became my medicine and my distraction from what I had been going through and what I had been missing. I called it love and needed it every day.

I felt like Chris Brown writing the song "Young Love". You couldn't tell me this wasn't love because it made me happy, so it had to be. Right?

Every night when we talked on the phone, it felt like we could talk about anything. We never talked about sex or anything like that though. We had never done anything more than a hug. That's how I knew he truly cared about me. All the older folks used to say, "if sex ain't the first thing he tryna do with you, it's love" and I believed it, even though sometimes he acted like he didn't want to be around me in public and would treat me differently in certain situations and places.

In middle school, I sang in the school choir. We would always have concerts, and one day, I asked him to come, and he did! But when I tried to introduce him to my mother, he pushed me away. I took it as him being nervous, so I laughed it off. The next day, we continued our regular routine, and it was like that for a while until we were on the phone one night and began talking about sex for the first and only time. When we got off the phone that night, we chose to continue that conversation through text and fell asleep.

The day after this conversation, I was ready for my regular dose of love "medicine" and forgot about the conversation we had the previous night. But when we got to school, he sat me down during our Engineering class and told me that his mother had looked through his phone and told him to break up with me. She didn't want him thinking about sex in the 8th grade, let alone talk about it. We were young black kids and statistically, teen pregnancy among African Americans was on a rise. Though the breakup was for a good reason, I didn't see it like that. I hated his mother. She stole the only ounce of love and sanity I had ever received from a man, and I hated her for it. I hated him too for listening to his mother and being obedient!

"Why can't you just lie and be rebellious like me??" I thought.

But he didn't. He broke up with me and left me as broken as I was when we first met.

That day, I came home heavy with the pain that I had carried the rest of that school day. I walked into the house, walked past my mother, went straight into my room, threw my bookbag on the floor, fell face forward on the bed, and wailed. I never knew that my heart could be so broken and that my small body could produce that many tears. But it did and like Drake said, "the first love is the sweetest, but that first cut is the deepest."

But was I truly grieving a heartbreak from this relationship, or was I mourning the loss of the thing that had been distracting me from the brokenness I had suffered earlier, at the hands of people like my father and the things I didn't want to pray about and face anymore?

Either way, he made me cry.

"She thought all she needed could be found in man
Building all her hopes and dreams on temporary
things
She's laughing on the outside but she's crying on the
inside she's
hangin' in there on a wing and a prayer and I can hear
her say…"
-    Fred Hammond

COUNTERFEITS, PLACEHOLDERS, SHAPESHIFTERS AND TEARS

My first "Placeholder" came quickly and unexpectedly to me. He came soon after the breakup.

Coincidence or blessing?

I took it as a blessing because I was able to forget about all the things I didn't want to face again. I was so happy but confused at the same time. This placeholder was close friends with the first guy who had made me cry. They called each other "brothers" to be exact. But did he know that his "brother" and I just broke up? I was confused but I went along with it and hoped my first love would notice and want me back.

My priorities started to change quickly. I went from worshipping and talking to God every day and beginning this amazing relationship with Him to jumping from one boy to another. Even though I was distracted by the boys, I still thought about God from time to time and knew I needed Him. I just wanted to feel more important to a boy, so I put God, my anger issues, unprocessed memories, feelings of being different and unloved, and the pain from my father's absence into a box in my mind and locked it all away. If anything else came up that I didn't want to face, I would lock that away too.

The new placeholder was an older boy who was in my oldest sister's class. He was the first older guy who showed interest in me. This made me feel superior.

"He could have any girl he wanted! But he chose me!" I thought.

Catching my first love's attention was an epic failure. The more he showed that I was nothing to him anymore, the more he became nothing to me. It also got easier because I had a distraction helping me to forget. I eventually chose to completely forget about him and us ever becoming an item again and focused on receiving the attention from his "brother."

Again, I was confused though. I felt pretty sometimes but overall, I was a short, skinny girl whose body wasn't developed yet. My hair wasn't that long or beautiful and to top it all off, I was an oddball. So why did he want me? How did I get a fine, older guy like him?
I felt like I was the "all that and a bag of chips" everybody referred to. I had hit the jackpot.

He never officially asked me to be his girlfriend like my first love did but we were very close to becoming an official couple. We talked every day and hung out more often than I was able to do with my first love. It was around summertime when we first started to hang out.

My neighborhood had a park that everyone went to, and I do mean everyone went to this park! If it wasn't to hang out with friends or fight, it was the spot for two people who liked each other to do things that they had no business doing. It became our hang-out spot, and he would always ask me to meet him there.

Around this time, I began to do whatever it took to defend whatever reality I created for myself, even if it was a false one. What do I mean? If I thought something was good for me, even if it wasn't, I would make it my reality, and if you threatened that reality, you were an enemy.

My oldest sister hated that a guy in her grade liked me and that I was hanging out with him. I felt like she was over-protective and that it wasn't her place to tell me who I could and couldn't see! I would fight with her, not over him, but to protect the reality I had created in my head about him. I fought to protect my false reality instead of addressing the red flags that I had started to notice about him.

It was a Saturday in the summertime and there was a huge group of us at our house. My sisters, friends from school, friends from up the street, and the Placeholder were all there at the house. We all decided to walk from our house to the park. As we walked, I could see from the corner of my eye that my sister did not like him being around at all. I rolled my eyes and slowed down. Everyone else continued walking in front of me but the Placeholder realized that I had slowed down, so he came to walk beside me.

"Can I kiss you?" He asked me.

My eyes got big, and I immediately said "yes!"

This was going to be my first kiss! I was so excited and ready to have this experience.

Everyone in the group was walking ahead but they all turned around at the exact moment he leaned in for the kiss.

My friends screamed in excitement as I felt like I was going through the rite of passage to becoming a woman.

He kissed me and everything in me lit up.

Even though his lips were a little dry, it didn't matter. I was happy. We separated after the kiss, and he went home as I ran to catch up with my sisters and friends. My oldest sister looked at me with disgust as everyone else cheered for me.

I always felt safer around the people who validated the reality I was protecting so I decided at that moment to stop talking to my oldest sister about him and bringing him around her.

We started meeting more in private and hanging out at the park by ourselves. The park was connected to a daycare that was only open in the daytime during the week. After six, no one was there, and that's when people started hanging out to do the exact thing, they had no business doing.

This was the first guy who introduced me to the curves of my body and showed me what a man's body looked like. We had never had sex because I was too afraid, and I didn't know what to do. This boy taught me everything but sex. I felt a different connection with him than I had with my first love.

"Is this real? Does he really care about me?" I questioned.

As a young black girl in the 8th grade, sex was the topic of many discussions along with drama. Someone always had an issue with someone, or someone was having sex with someone. That was just the reality at school. Nothing was off-topic, and no one was safe from the drama.

"This boy is in high school, and I'm pretty sure he has done everything he's showing and introducing me to, with someone else. He must have a hidden agenda 'cause, why me?" I kept thinking.

"But he chose me, right?" I continued.

Every time I had those thoughts, I locked them away in that box with God and the other things and lived in the moment. I was happy!

One Friday evening, a friend of mine texted me and asked if I was still talking to the Placeholder. She was one of the people in the large group at the park with us the day I got my first kiss. I responded immediately and said "yes." She asked me what his last name was. I responded and told her.

"Kayla, he has a girlfriend," she texted back.

My jaw dropped.

"What?!? How do you know?" I responded quickly, still in shock.

At that time in school, if you had a phone, a popular thing people had been signatures. When you would text people, your unique signature would get sent along with the message. My friend said that the Placeholder's last name was the signature of one of her friends. She gave me the girl's number to see the signature for myself and to talk to her directly.

I did and I let him go immediately right after that.

This was my first time being in such a situation. I felt so used, betrayed, lied to, and angry. All I could do was cry. Again.

This series of situationships started to create a monster inside of me. I added this pain, heartbreak, betrayal, and embarrassment to that box in the back of my mind and tucked it all away. The box got fuller and heavier. I didn't want to talk to God, but I knew I needed to.

I knew I needed to talk to God because I couldn't run to anyone else. I didn't want to talk with my sisters because one seemed like she didn't care, and the other had been right about this Placeholder, and I hated being wrong. My mother worked a lot, and I really didn't want to talk to her about any of these things, so I kept it all to myself. By choosing to do that, anger became the only emotion I could resort to. I was angry at everything and became extremely aggressive until I came to God, crying one day in my room.

"Why is everything so hard?"

I started telling Him how angry I was. I couldn't control my father being in and out of my life. I couldn't change the things that had already happened.

"I HATE YOU!" I screamed, angry because of the hardships and my circumstances.

"Nobody understands me! No one has ever understood me, and the only thing that makes me happy is being in a relationship! And every time I think he's the one, you take that from me!" I screamed at Him.

I cried myself to sleep that night and decided to not care anymore about anything or anyone. That night, I died a little inside.

When I thought things couldn't get worse, they did.

Time passed and I went from one guy to the next, heartbreak after heartbreak, one placeholder to another, and I was tired.

I eventually went back to try to fix my relationship with God. I was ready to give it another shot so I decided to get baptized. Even though I felt like I didn't need to because I still remembered the day, I gave my life to Him in that bathroom when I was a little girl, I just wanted to make it official.

Nothing was different this particular Sunday except me. It was August and my family, and I were at church sitting in our regular spots. I leaned over to Marchea, one of my sisters, and asked her if she would walk up to the front with me when the "door of the church opened," which was when new members and those who wanted to get baptized would present themselves at the front of the church. My sister was shyer than me at this age, so if anyone needed emotional support, it would be her, not me but I asked anyway. Nonetheless, my sister agreed to go up with me so I wouldn't be alone since I was afraid and didn't know what to expect. I just wanted to be baptized.

Service ended and the doors of the church finally opened. I nudged my sister to let her know that I was ready to go to the front. As we both got up and walked towards the front of the church, I heard clapping all around me. My mom and Mamo began to cry and two women who were in the front of the church started to walk towards us to embrace us.

"Do you both want to join the church today?" One of the women asked my sister and me.

"Yes," we both answered. I looked over at my sister, shocked because I thought she only came up with me to support me, not because she was thinking of getting baptized too.

We stayed after church to discuss the dates of our baptism. We chose August 11th which was in three weeks. Suddenly, I felt good again.

I felt like that little girl coming out of the bathroom that day when I was first introduced to God. I was happy and hopeful again... until I wasn't.

I started to notice that every time I would take one step closer to God, distractions in the form of my deepest desires would appear. If I couldn't have my father, I wanted the closest thing to the love he was supposed to give me, which I only found in relationships with boys. I found myself in situations with boys who were just as broken as me. We made commitments to fill the voids in each other until one of us was done, which usually ended up being them, most of the time.

Then came another boy. He was the first "Counterfeit" that I encountered. He was new and was from the other side of town. He and his family moved into one of the houses up the street from mine. We were the same age and grade. I honestly didn't think too much of him, but I knew he was very fond of me and would do anything it took to show me that he liked me. He was very different from the rest of the guys I had ever liked. He was extremely goofy, nerdy, and lowkey irritating. My mom didn't like him much either, but he went to church, which was what got my attention. It was his form of Godliness that caught my eye because I had been trying to get my life together around that time.

I kind of had to force myself to like him and get attracted to him at first but I got over it because of the attention he gave me. I could have just been honest and not dated him because I didn't really like him, but instead, I took advantage of the fact that he liked me so much and made me feel important and a priority.

It was around this time in my life that I began to flip the script and started using men. I was tired of the tears and broken hearts. I had already started the habit of tucking away the things I didn't want to face and so when I was given the opportunity to feel like I was in control, I gladly took it, and a monster was born in me. This combination became my drug. Instead of addressing my problem, I went on pretending like I really liked him.

We started dating right before my baptism. I chose to believe that God had His hands on the situation just because I considered this new guy, "a church boy."

Not too long after we started dating, my sister and I got baptized and my mindset changed. I felt reset and more refreshed. I felt like everything I had done and gone through in the past had been removed, but I had very little understanding of what I was doing or what was supposed to happen afterward. I just wanted to feel something different from the hopelessness of a never-ending cycle. I thought baptism would change that for me, but it didn't because I was ignorant to what this relationship and journey with God were supposed to look like. I felt like I was digging myself into a deeper hole and it started to have a snowball effect.

Not even a week had gone by when I fell into this thing no one ever really talked to me about, called sin. I gave my virginity to the Counterfeit. I was a 14-year-old little girl, and I gave my innocence away. I wasn't just emotionally tangled anymore, now I was physically invested too. He was the first boy that I gave my body to, so what I was feeling before, I was now feeling it 10 times more. I became more connected to him than I was before. I became extremely sensitive to everything he said and did from then on. I wasn't familiar with soul ties or what it even meant. I just thought this was love. It was as if I went from one drug to another. I went from filling my voids with meaningless relationships to now sex.

Sex put my mind in a fantasy. Whatever the reality was didn't matter anymore because I was on a constant high. I got addicted immediately but not to him, to the feeling he gave me through sex. I began to be hyper-fixated on this one thing, to the point that I didn't care about the relationship or him anymore, just the sex. Again, I called this love.

He ended up becoming my longest relationship and the only one with whom I was intimate. Later, the form of Godliness that I thought I saw in him started to become exposed. He wasn't who he portrayed himself to be. He was just a boy who went to church because his family was in the church. But was I any better? I was the one who had initiated sex with him.

The feeling of guilt for having sex with him was starting to overwhelm me, so I decided to tell my mother. I chose to tell her in church where she couldn't hit me. I looked at my mother as I sat next to her in church and told her that I had to tell her something. She looked at me with a strong gaze that pierced my soul and right away, she said "you had sex?"

I looked back at her with puppy eyes and hurriedly responded "yes." Even though she couldn't hit me because we were in church, I was so scared!

She looked away and told me she would deal with me later.

When we got home, she pulled me into the room and asked me two questions:

1. "Did you use protection?"

2. "Did he force you?"

I answered laughing because I was so shocked that this was the only thing she was worried about. I answered her by saying, "yes we used protection" but laughed even more when answering the last question. "No Mommy, he didn't force me. I was the one who initiated it. If anything, I forced him!"

We grew and stayed in the relationship and decided that we were going to get married one day. All this was because of the voids we were able to fill up in each other. It was trauma bonding, but we were calling it love. The only reason we were together for so long was because we were convenient for each other and that made us important to each other.

We lasted for almost a year until his sister told him to break up with me. She had been drunk one day and we got into an argument, so she made him choose between me or her. Of course with that being his sister, he chose her.

During this time in my life, I would feel pain a little bit, but I had begun getting numb to a lot of things in life. I wasn't responding to things as a regular 14-year-old girl. It was because I wasn't a regular 14-year-old girl, and I began to just accept that.

One night, not too long after the breakup with the Counterfeit, I decided to sneak out. Now, sneaking out and running away at this point in my life wasn't unusual. It was extremely common. I would do it all the time with one of my best friends, Deja. My mother worked the third shift and Mamo and Papo slept downstairs so most of the time, I got away with sneaking out.

This night she had fallen asleep. I was up and I just wanted to leave the house
so I messaged a handful of people on my phone to see if they were up to just walk around the neighborhood with me. That night was the first night I encountered the first "Shapeshifter". He was one of the people I had texted.

He texted me back right away and said he would meet me outside my house in about 10 minutes. Ready to just leave the house and escape for a little while, I gladly hopped out the window and waited outside my house. He arrived and we started walking and talking. He asked me if I was still in a relationship and how that was going. I told him we weren't together anymore, and he started asking questions on what happened and how long ago etc. Thinking he really cared, I went on a rant, explaining what had happened from beginning to end. Mid-story however, I noticed that we had ended up by his house. He asked me to come to his house with him.

I was oblivious to his true intentions for wanting to sneak out with me in the first place, but his reason was now as clear as day and right in front of my face. I brushed it off, said "no" and kept walking and talking. We ended up back in front of my house and I thanked him. Right before I could follow up with a goodbye, he asked if he could walk me closer to the house. We walked by the side of my house and as I began explaining to him how I used the stool on the side of my house to lift myself into my window, he grabbed me, trying to kiss me. In full confusion, I said "no!" while trying to snatch away from him. He was stronger so he was able to push me up against the side of my house as he pulled down my pants and panties at the same time. He told me to let him "eat me out" as he pinned me to the wall. Terrified, I stood there in shock and didn't move.

A car drove past slowly with bright lights and for some reason, that caused him to stop. If that car hadn't gone by, I don't know what would have happened.

I knew exactly what would have happened, but it was easier to lie to myself saying I didn't know.

He ran away and texted me later asking me not to tell anyone and that he had been drunk.

I sat outside and cried. I needed to tell someone, so I texted my ex-boyfriend. I told him what had happened, but his immediate response was …

"Why are you out hanging with a boy this late anyway?"

"That's what you get for being with him."

I stopped replying to his messages and went inside, hoping to find comfort in one of my sisters. I got inside and went to my sisters' room and tapped my oldest sister on the shoulder. "Briana, BRIANA!"

"What?" She spoke.

"Can I sleep with you, please?"

"No, Kayla, why?"

"Please, I don't wanna talk about it. Please just let me sleep with you tonight. "

"No Kayla!"

"I just snuck out with Shapeshifter. He almost raped me, and I'm really scared."

She looked at me, told me that it didn't happen, and told me to go to my room and go to sleep.

I did exactly what my sister told me to do, and I shoved that experience to the deepest part of the box in my mind and went to sleep, believing it didn't happen and that it was all my fault. My anxious body stopped shaking.

Before that day, only some of me was numb but after that day, I became completely numb. Another part of me died that night.

A few months passed. I was still in school and the girl that my first Placeholder cheated on me with, and I had become friends! She was cool, and we got along well. We began hanging out all the time and started becoming something like best friends. She and I both had no dealings with the Placeholder and had both moved on. I was still single, but she had a boyfriend.

She had been arguing for a couple of days with her boyfriend, who lived in another part of town and went to a different school. He was cousins with the boy who would become the second Shapeshifter.

My friend's boyfriend was finally in town and was at his cousin's house. She asked me to walk over to the house with her because she didn't want to walk over there alone. I understood and would have asked someone to do the same for me if I was in the same situation. As a matter of fact, I had already been in situations where I had asked a friend or two to come with me to places so I wouldn't be alone. I knew things would be fine because we knew him and his cousin plus it was in the middle of the day, so we had enough time to go there for them to talk and hang out and then walk home before it got dark to prepare for school the next day.

We arrived at the cousin's house and she and her boyfriend went downstairs to talk which left me alone with the cousin whom I knew... or so I thought. We were going to the same school. He and I were in some classes together and I also knew he liked me. He was cool and I did find him attractive, but I was still hoping things were going to work out with the Counterfeit. I had hoped we would get back together, so my heart and mind were not in a place of looking for a new relationship.

As they went downstairs, the cousin showed me around his house, making small talk and being very kind, again... so I thought. He invited me into his room because he had said that he wanted to show me something. I walked into the room, and he shut the door behind us. He invited me to sit on his bed. I sat on the corner of the bed, and we began talking. He then began touching my face and body, letting me know that he wanted to be sexual. Without directly asking, he started kissing me. I said "no!" trying to push him off me. Because he was so much taller and bigger than me, he was able to use his strength to pin me down to the bed. I tried getting up, but he would pin me down every time, trying to have his way. Because of all the movement, his door cracked open a little, so I bit his arm, kicked him from me, and ran out the door to look for my friend. It was time to go. I ran downstairs to look for her, just to walk in on her and her boyfriend having sex. I ran back upstairs and flew out the front door.

I walked home alone that day and I didn't tell anyone what had happened either. I didn't want to hear the same things I had heard last time when this happened, so like everything else, I put it in the box and did what I had been doing this whole time, which was, avoid the truth and try to fill voids.

Imagine what I had turned into by this time with everything that had happened. I had been doing this since I was little. I tried God but it seemed like He never showed up unless it was Sunday morning in a church building, but I needed him on Hamlet Rd, at my house and it just didn't seem like He was there, so I did what I needed to do to survive.

The monster inside of me grew. I became extremely promiscuous. I continued going from one guy to the next, one trauma bond to the next, having sex with men who shared similar characteristics or who were extremely older. That made me feel mature for my age, even though I was as immature as the next person. I was being used and mistreated and I was doing the same to them. I was just trying to survive.

That's when God sent me an angel. The church I had always been going to, hired a new Pastor. He had a wife and two children and when he came, a lot of things changed. With everything I had been going through, I was still in church. I was involved in the church as well. My sisters and I pretty much did everything in the church. I committed myself to ministry before I ever truly committed myself to God and it showed.

My sisters and I were a part of the dance ministry at the church until he came and changed some things around. The dance ministry ended and when it did, it was like the only thing left that gave me life was taken away.

My sisters and I couldn't stop dancing. We were asked to participate in our aunt's youth program at her church. Being asked to do something like that birthed our dance ministry, "His Callin." My sisters and I had started dancing in the church a little before the experience I had had with my mother in the bathroom, where she told me about God.

This was my life in the church house but at home, it was hell. As I got older and had more undealt-with trauma, I became the main issue in my home. I was the one who argued with everyone. I was the one who would walk out of the house with no explanation and not come back for hours or until the next day. I would blow up and cuss everyone out. My mother had three go-to threats when I got to that point:

1. "I'm going to send you with your father."
2. "I'm going to put you on "Beyond Scared Straight.""
3. "I'm going to put you in therapy."

My response to each of those was:
1. It didn't move me. If my father wasn't here before by choice, why in the world would she

expect him to be here now for me when my behavior was the direct result of his absence.

2.   Still didn't move me. How in the world could she afford to put me on this show when we were on government assistance and could barely afford to make it each day?

3.   This was the threat that made me tighten up. I was scared to be labeled as crazy so I would always either cry or beg her. She would respond by telling me to get it together or that would be the next step. I was so afraid of the misconception of therapy at that time but if I had known what I know now, I would have understood that this was exactly what I needed.

When things got too bad or beyond repair, after I had one of my blowups and ran away, my mother would call my first angel, my uncle, to find me and pick me up. I needed a father, and he was everything I needed and more when he came through, and he always came through. He wouldn't ask me questions about what happened. He would just pick me up, take me to his house and let me do what I needed to do, whether it was to escape for a while or talk about whatever it was that I wanted to talk about.

Most of the time we would sleep, watch movies or I would play and hang out with my cousins or just play with his dog. He and his house were my safe place.

Dancing kept me sane and focused. I didn't have as many episodes when I danced. This was the gift that God used to help save my life and sanctify me unknowingly. The lyrics to the songs were seeds being planted in my mind and spirit, causing me to submit to God without me even realizing it. When I danced to these songs, my body became the message that was being delivered to the people that I was ministering to. I was the bridge between the song and the people. I was the vessel being used to deliver whatever message God had for His people. By being the vessel and dancing to these songs, my life slowly started to change.

After ministering for the first time under our own dance ministry, many people contacted my mother asking us to dance for their churches, programs, plays, and services. We began going everywhere and being used by God, but the main place where we were being used was our home church. The new Pastor was extremely fond of my sisters and me and we started getting close to him because of that.

He first formed a relationship with our mother and began sharing with her that he felt called to my sisters and me. He started forming a relationship with all three of us by simply taking us individually to Starbucks on Saturday mornings.

He couldn't really get close to my oldest sister, Briana, because not too long after he started meeting with us, she had to start preparing for college, so she was extremely occupied. My middle sister, Marchea, didn't connect with people much at that time, especially men, so that didn't go anywhere.

Then he met me, the one he said he felt called to the most. Many people have said that to me. When I danced, I used those moments to deal with my issues and the things I didn't want to face head-on so you would see so much passion and power. It could move the most still person, but the Pastor saw beyond that and saw a broken little girl.

When we had our first meeting, I had just broken up with another Counterfeit that I dated in the church. He was just another church boy who had a form of Godliness but no evidence of God, just like me. He cheated on me with a girl at his school and I found out. It confused me because he had given me his virginity and I thought you had deep connections with your first. It wasn't enough apparently, because he still cheated, and again, I was ready to find another Placeholder to fill the void.

He picked me up around 10 am and took me to Starbucks. That first conversation, I told him EVERYTHING that was going on. I told him how the Counterfeit hurt me, how I hated home and how I hated school. I was miserable. I told him how my father wasn't there and how it had affected me. I told him how I wanted a relationship with God, but it felt like He didn't want a relationship with me. I felt safe and I felt like he heard me. I didn't really trust men during that time so there was a lot of pushback at first but at that moment, I just wanted to be heard. I told him that maybe I was miserable because of the prayer I had prayed.

He asked me what the prayer was. I told him that I was so tired of my own cycles and the things I was going through that I had asked God to put destruction in my life to get me in order.

He looked at me with both eyebrows raised as if I had cussed him out directly. He took a sip of coffee and laughed an uncomfortable laugh.

"Ughh what made you ask God this?"

I told him I didn't know. I brushed it off and kept talking.

He and I met every two weeks after that and formed a bond.

Around that time, God also reconnected my sisters and me to a woman who used to go to our church at one time. She and her husband loved us and wanted to stay connected to us. My mother gave her the role of our Godmother. She had started picking up my sisters and me on some weekends, to spend time with us before the new Pastor came along. Around the time we started meeting and forming a relationship with him, she started a Christian mentorship program for young girls called "Gladiolus."

Gladiolus was a beautiful flower. Our Godmother's vision and heart were for young girls from broken or in broken situations, to bring love and order to us so we could bloom and become beautiful flowers. The flower looked like a sword with petals, and it represented honor, courage, and faithfulness. These were the foundational characteristics of this program for young girls. We met every month, had retreats, and annual ceremonies for the ones who were graduating and going to college. It truly blessed us.

With our dance ministry moving forward, meeting every two weeks with the Pastor, going through this program, and having my uncle always on standby, I finally felt like I was going in the right direction with my life. I was becoming a less problematic teenager and building a stronger relationship with God.

One Saturday night, I was laying down in bed listening to the song "My Testimony" by Marvin Sapp. "His Callin" was going to minister to this song at our home church the next day. The night before we would minister, I would always put the song on repeat on my phone and let it minister to me and sing over me. That night, I fell asleep with the headphones in my ears. God gave me a dream.

The dream was taking place at our home church where we were supposed to minister that Sunday. My sisters and I were dancing to "My Testimony" with a fully packed church. As we did a particular dance move, we turned to our right and everyone in the church pews and pulpit vanished. I screamed to alarm my sisters and told them "RUN!" because on the side we had turned while doing that dance move, I saw Satan. I didn't see his face, but I knew it was him. He was wearing an all-black cloak with a hood that covered his face. When I screamed "RUN!", he quickly approached me and tried to get me. As I tried to run, I turned my body, and immediately saw my Jesus. He ran up in front of me pushing me and stood face to face with the Devil.

I had that same dream repeatedly until I woke up, hyperventilating and sweating.

I told my mother the dream and what had happened. She looked at me and told me that though I was taking steps in the right direction, the Devil was still trying to get my attention and will, but Jesus was fighting for me.

My next meeting with the Pastor came and I was eager to tell him my dream and see what he had to say.

He came and picked me up as usual but had a different demeanor that Saturday morning. He would always crack jokes, be silly and goofy but that day, he had a more serious demeanor. It was like something was going on. He told me we were going to get breakfast instead of our regular Starbucks run and that he had to talk with me when we got there.

To say I was afraid in my heart was an understatement. A regular person would have taken this a little differently, but I had recently been diagnosed with anxiety disorder at my last doctor's visit. They had wanted to put me on medication, but my mother refused. Maybe medication would have helped me calm down at that moment. My mind began thinking of all kinds of worst-case scenarios.

"He's going to leave."

"I did something wrong, and now he's going to leave me."

"I disappointed him and he's going to leave me."

I was so quiet in the car thinking these things, trying to prepare myself for him to tell me that he was leaving me, that the thing I was so eager to talk to him about before became a distant memory.

We arrived at the restaurant, ordered our food and he looked at me and said "Kayla."

"Yes sir" I answered.

"I want to share something with you." He said as he looked directly into my eyes

I had always been uncomfortable with eye contact, especially from a man so I began to try and look away.

"God has called me to step into your life and be your father. I have already talked to your mother, and she said yes. Would you allow me to be your father?"

I had prayed for this and didn't even realize it was happening. I couldn't articulate a response.

I was still in shock and had not been able to speak when he began to speak over my life, telling me that I was called to do great things in this life. He told me that my ministry was going to be bigger than a specific church. He said that he saw me being restored and helping many people.

Again, I was still confused but it made me feel good. That was the first time anyone ever saw that much in me.

He continued, saying that I needed to put a pause on relationships and find who I was. He told me that I had to heal and let go of things from my past. He told me that God had a great thing for me to do but being in relationship after relationship wasn't going to help.

"Kayla, you are called to do so much in the Kingdom. Do not get in a relationship with a man who doesn't see or know that. You are not meant to be with a man who wants to keep you in a house. If that ever happens, leave immediately."

I responded, "yes sir". I also answered "yes" to receive him as my father.

I tried to prepare him by telling him how much of a mess I was and that I was difficult and brought so much trouble because that was all I knew of myself. I didn't see me the way he saw me, and I wanted to prepare him before he got disappointed. He just looked at me and told me that he knew and that he was ordained by God to be my father and to stop and let him father me.

I wanted to see myself through his eyes more and kept trying to ask questions because it brought me so much joy. He told me that my identity is not in what he saw or said, but in God. He told me to ask God who I was and to ask Him to help me be that. He told me not to rely on the words of man.

That conversation changed my life and perspective forever.

From that day forward, I tried my best to not get into relationships with guys but if I did, I had to truly like them and if things didn't work out, I took the initiative and broke up with them and moved on. I continued going through the Gladiolus program, learning healthier and authentic ways to help me become the woman I believe God wanted me to be. I continued my relationship with the people I called my spiritual mothers and fathers. I began trying to practice celibacy and my dance ministry with my sisters thrived.

Years passed and I graduated high school and started having the desire to walk in more of the woman I believed God wanted me to be. I learned that I loved speaking and I loved educating people on things and topics that were beneficial to them. I asked God to help me with becoming who He had called me to be, and He gave me direction.

God directed me to go to college after I graduated High School. Though I already wanted to, I was scared and even though my sisters were both in college and I had someone to look up to, I knew I would go down a different path than my sisters and that I would be alone. God directed me to go to a private Bible College. Because I was barely doing well in high school, I was very skeptical of them accepting me due to my low GPA and ACT/SAT scores.

At the beginning of my senior year, I felt the desire to go to the same Bible College that God had directed me to go to, but they told me that they didn't believe women could preach and that women had to take different courses than men. I was mad about that and said "no", but God said "yes."

In fear, I decided to apply to the college where both of my sisters were going to but right when I did that, my oldest sister told me that my journey would be different. God had a different plan for me than her and my other sister, so she told me not to come to their college.

In faith, I applied and got conditionally accepted into the Bible college, which meant I had until the first semester to prove myself capable and ready for college.

I had already made up my mind to surpass that goal because I wanted to learn the Bible and become who God wanted me to be, more than anything else in the world.
I came into college in a relationship with a guy who was just another Counterfeit, another man who had a form of Godliness but again, no fruit.

But as I allowed college to transform me, my taste in men started to change. I broke up with my boyfriend because I wanted a man like the men I was seeing in school. Most of these men were on fire for God and desired marriage, like me. I wanted a man like my spiritual father, a Pastor who bore fruit and wanted to do the will of God, but I still had major issues due to unresolved trauma and other things that I had to unlearn. I was still choosing the same type of man. I chose men who had potential but not the full package.

 I later learned that I had altered my mind so much by dismissing reality, that I didn't know what the truth was anymore. I lived in a constant state of fantasy. I overlooked red flags, toxic behaviors, and dangerous habits that could potentially put me in danger. I was traumatized and going to church and praying wasn't enough anymore. I was tired of the same old cycles, but I wasn't willing to change.

I knew all these things to be true when I dated another guy towards the end of my freshman year of college. He was different from the rest, and I was really attracted to him. We became friends by working together and having a couple of the same classes. After I broke up with my last boyfriend, I set my heart on dating a believer, but this guy gave me everything I ever wanted. He just wasn't a believer, but I didn't care. I liked him anyway.

I was full of myself. I would take a couple of steps forward in my life and think I had arrived, even though I didn't do any real work on myself.

I was doing the best I had ever done in school and had all A's and B's. I started a Bible Study for women in college. I was working a great job and had gotten another job for the summer. I was hired as the Creative Arts Director at the Salvation Army downtown and my new boyfriend got a job working there as well. My boyfriend was also on the basketball team and was one of the best players on the team.

We were about two months into our relationship when he told me that I was his wife and asked my mother for my hand in marriage. After work one day, we hopped on the bus and went to the bank to open a joint bank account to prepare for our wedding day. Everything was perfect in my eyes, and I felt like I had finally arrived, not knowing that pride came right before the fall.

As the Creative Arts Director, I was given the responsibility of teaching music, dance, and arts. I also had to come up with or find a play for the kids and staff to participate in during the summer program. With limited time, I wanted to go with the easier route of finding a play to learn and teach the kids, but God was moving me in a different direction. God led me to write my first play called "When you surrender all." We called it a "Hip Hopera" because my boyfriend and one of the other directors were writers and rappers as well. We all came together, writing songs, scripts and planning for this big event that was not too far away.

The "Hip Hopera" was about 4 kids who were all in different situations and decided to give their life to God.

The first child was a boy who became a believer but had parents who weren't believers. The second was a girl who gave her life to God and had a boyfriend who wasn't a believer. The next was a boy who had grown up in the church and had a lukewarm family, but he wanted to be really about Jesus. The last girl was an older girl who took care of her younger siblings because there was no parent, and she was paving the way for her family. They all became leaders at a young age by taking the stand to be ambassadors of Jesus Christ and they went through warfare because of it.

The kids sang songs and rapped. It was my first-time teaching dance ministry to children, and it was a large group of children. They got out of their comfort zones and truly made this Hip Hopera come alive.

As we came to the last week of preparing for the Grand Opening of "When You Surrender All", my boyfriend and I were struggling and had been going through a lot. He had become distant, and I didn't understand why but on the night of the grand opening, he seemed fine until after it was all over. I asked him if he could take me home and he said no. I was confused so I pulled him to the side and asked him what was going on.

He told me that he had to break up with me because he was entering his senior year and had to focus on himself.

"I thought I was your wife?" I responded, shocked and angry.

He pulled out some money from his wallet and gave it to me.

"What is this?!" I said furiously.

He said it was my half of the money that I had put in our joint bank account. He had closed the account and was giving the money back to me.

I went off! I started screaming and yelling with tears rolling down my face. I threw the money at his face!

"WHY? WHY ARE YOU DOING THIS?"

He looked at me with tears in his eyes and said, "God told me to leave you alone. He told me you weren't my wife."

I thought I was loud before, but I got louder, and I threw and broke my phone. He walked away that day with my sanity. I lost it after that.

Every day was grey skies and long nights. Now I was not only dealing with anxiety, but I was dealing with depression too.

It was August and I was two weeks away from moving into my college dorm to prepare for my sophomore year. I had received a full-ride scholarship for the rest of my college year, and it required me to live on campus.

I had a broken heart, anxiety, depression and I was now pissed at God. Life didn't stop though. I still had bills to pay. I still had to go to school, and I had to move on even though at that time, a part of me was still stuck on my ex-boyfriend and that Saturday night when he had broken up with me.

As school started, I felt like I should drop the semester. It was the hardest time of my life thus far. Every day, I felt like I was dragging myself to class. Every day, I was forcing myself to eat. Most days, I didn't even eat. I was in the deepest depression that I had ever experienced in my life. I just wanted the pain to go away. I needed the pain to go away.

Around this time, I was introduced to Travis Greene and his music. He had a song on his newest album called "Love Me Too Much." This song ministered to me so much and blessed me beyond measure. The song talked about how amazing God is and that He loves us too much to leave us where we are.

I was so blinded by the fantasy and false reality that I created in my head, that I didn't even realize that God was fulfilling the prayer I had prayed when I asked Him to put destruction in my life to get me in order. Although I had noticed the mess that I had become and was tired, I wasn't done living life my way or for myself.

The full-ride scholarship called the Urban Scholar scholarship that I had gotten, provided so much more than just relief from the financial stress that came with college. It connected me with a community of people that helped me throughout my college career. I met so many well-known and gifted people of God.

That is how I met him. He was a placeholder, counterfeit, and shapeshifter all in one.

"He [God] is not caught off guard by any of our life
situations.
Everything,
The hardships, the trials, the storm
It's not happening to us; it's happening for us,
because our God is intentional."
- Travis Greene

TO THE BREAKING THEN TRANSITION

I had known him since the previous school year. I was going to a predominantly white college so there were few black kids on campus. All the students who had the Urban Scholars Scholarship were in the BIPOC community (Black, Indigenous, or People of Color) so we were naturally drawn to each other. He as well had the scholarship.

Coming into my sophomore year of college, I noticed that he and I had a science class together. Because I was dealing with heartbreak and depression, entering the school year was extremely rough for me. I also didn't have a job. At that point in time, I still didn't have my license or a car. I was struggling inwardly and outwardly.

One day in class, while answering a question, he had mentioned something about his job and that they were hiring. He was working at a school in an afterschool program under a grant funded by the government. The program was working with kids from K-6 grade. With me just coming out of the summer working as a Creative Arts Director and with kids in that same age range, I felt more than capable of doing the job. I went to him after class that day and asked him about the job and if he could potentially put a good word in for me. He did just that and I got the job. Because I didn't have a car or a license, he agreed to take me to and from work with him.

I didn't talk with him much outside of work and class because I was still going through the motions of heartache, plus I still wasn't looking for anyone else. I was hoping my ex would come back to me.

October rolled around and I found out that my ex-boyfriend had not only moved on, but he had a new girlfriend. Even though I was devastated, I felt released from the mental bondage of wondering if he would ever come back. Obviously, he had no plans to.

Now dealing with the hardest heartbreak I had ever experienced in my life and having so much trauma stored up, I was breaking, and I was vulnerable. I constantly felt like I was losing my mind. I kept talking about him and our breakup because I seriously couldn't get over it. Everyone around me was so tired of me, but I couldn't help it.

One night after "Family", a weekly service at my college, I began talking to some guys I trusted and considered my brothers. That night, one of my brothers opened my eyes forever when he told me that I was "broken." He told me to open the Bible app and look up Jeremiah 2:13 which reads

> "My people have committed two sins:
> They have forsaken me,
> the spring of living water,
> and have dug their own cisterns,
> broken cisterns that cannot hold water."

This Scripture spoke so much to me that I was moved to tears. This is what I had been doing this whole time, my whole life. I had been putting my trust and faith in broken people, people who were just as broken as me, expecting them to hold me up but instead we would end up hurting each other in the end.

That night, out of love, he told me that I was broken and that I needed to seek God to make me whole. Even though it was the truth, and I was tired, I still wasn't done but it moved me so much that I got that Scripture tattooed on my lower right arm to remember that night. I continued to do what I wanted to do because it felt better than facing the truth.

As this new guy and I began being around each other more and more, I started to notice that he noticed me. I didn't look at him as more than a friend. I didn't find him attractive, and I really didn't like him until one day, as I was in my dorm room with some of my friends, he called. He asked me if I wanted any food. Because I had him on speaker, all my friends heard and went bonkers! They were excited for me because they had noticed how he looked at me as well. I told them how I felt towards him and one of my friends responded with an alternative perspective, saying that a lot of times we don't find the people we end up in a relationship with attractive at first, that doesn't mean one day we won't grow into liking them.

Impressed with the quality of that response, I started to look at things differently from that point on.

After getting food, I asked him if he knew any good churches to go to. He suggested his church and that they had a service at 10:30 am on Sundays. I was excited because he paid for the food, and I was also excited to get back into church. Even more exciting was finding out that he believed in God and that he was in church. He was more involved in the church than any other guy I had ever dated. He was not only involved in his home church, but he was involved in other churches as well. He was a well-known drummer, and he was super musically talented.

Some time passed after the first time we went to church together and it was clear that what I was saying before didn't match my actions. It was clear to everyone that I had started liking him the way he liked me. One morning before heading to one of my classes, my roommate and best friend at the time told me that she had a dream about this new guy and me.

"I don't think you should do this," she said to me.

"Do what?" I asked in response.

She said, "you and this Shapeshifter."

"Why?" I asked in disappointment.

I wanted to believe my husband had finally found me. My aches and pains from the last boyfriend had finally stopped and I felt like I deserved to be happy, no matter what anyone had to say.

"I had a dream that you guys were in his car. He was angry and you were both fighting," she continued with sincere concern.

It was known that this Shapeshifter had trouble controlling his anger. This was something he was aware of himself and had already told me. I just didn't think it was that serious, just like the dream. I felt like she said this because a week prior, he and I had what I considered to be a small disagreement.

Around the anniversary of the death of his father, he would not only be depressed but be suicidal too. This was that time of the year. I didn't know that he was grieving at the time. He had asked me to bring him some liquid soap when we met up which I did. We met in a room in our college lounge and during our conversation, I said something that offended him. He took the soap, threw it towards the door, pushed me, and stormed off.

My roommate and another friend of mine were the ones I called when it happened. I was on the floor in tears. When I explained what had happened, they told me how dangerous it sounded.

"He put his hands on you?" One of my friends asked.

"No, I made him upset. It was my fault." I responded.

That was my first-time covering things up for him. I lied for two reasons. I didn't want people to see the truth about him. I wanted to fix him before it was exposed, and I wanted this relationship to work. I didn't care how jacked up it looked. I refused to go through the same pain I went through with my ex-boyfriend before him, the guy I really thought I was going to marry.

I tucked this situation and the dream my friend had far away in the back of my mind along with the things in my past.

Before I knew it, we were hanging out every day and I was going to church with him every Sunday. Us working together also brought us closer together. By November, he and I were intentionally dating. We weren't in a relationship yet, but we were close to it.

We made it official, but it was like God was making it clear from the beginning, with red flags, that I needed to leave. I had only experienced Shapeshifters who would change their faces in front of me but with him, I saw how he shifted, morphed, and changed faces in front of other people and in different settings. It was like God's mercy was on me. Even though I rejected the dream and the covert abusive behavior towards me, He continued to show me signs.

I just mastered disregarding the red flags.

The end of that school year came quickly. I was becoming a junior in college, and he was preparing to finally graduate that year. He was supposed to have graduated the year before but due to reasons he never shared with me, he had to go through another year. He wasn't prepared for life after college and things were not working out the way he had wanted them to at the time.

Though he did graduate, post-graduation depression was his reality just like it was for many others.

I was in a different part of my life though. I got a great job working as an intern in the youth department at a church. My goal that summers was to get a car and get my license.

This is where I started noticing that his true colors were beginning to show. He had already expressed that he had always battled with depression, but he started opening more about why. He had experienced different traumatic experiences growing up such as losing his father as a pre-teen and witnessing violence in his home. He talked about how these things affected him greatly. He expressed that he didn't want to become what he had seen or what he had been through.

The contradiction, however, was that while opening and talking about these things, he began shifting into the exact person that he didn't want to be, right in front of me.

I tried to be understanding and support him because I loved him, so I began educating myself on mental illnesses. It was during that process and while studying Psychology as my major in school that my love and deep desire to learn more about mental health and emotional intelligence was born.

During that time was also when the covert abuse began. Covert abuse is any type of underhanded, and not openly displayed abuse. It started off as blow-ups, punching holes in walls and breaking doors.

When I was working as an intern at the church, I lived with a host family. It was just a woman who had room for another intern and me to live upstairs of her house for the duration of the internship. She offered her house to us, interns because she was a partner of the church and she believed in the work that was being done to bring Jesus to the community.

One day, the Shapeshifter came over to hang out and bought some drinks because he wanted to drink that day. In that hard season of his life, he sometimes smoked and used substances such as alcohol. He would get irritable faster so we would argue a lot more for no reason and later that day, that is exactly what happened. There was an argument. He got angry, blew up, and tried to push me out of the way to leave the house. Afraid the owner of the house would see him angry, I tried to calm him down so that when he got downstairs, no one would know that something had happened. Trying to calm him down backfired. He threw me down on the ground, punched a hole in the wall, and left. My response at that moment, and at the earlier stages of the covert abuse, was to cry and shut down and when people asked, I covered for him. I lied and in situations like this one, I would even pay for the damages.

For about four more months after that situation, this was the routine:

1. I would do something that would make him upset or respond to something he did.
2. He would blow up.
3. He would break something or damage something.
4. I would freeze/shut down and cry.

At that time, he was still living with his mother and their relationship began to be stressful because she expected more from him. Their relationship started to become unhealthy because he didn't know how to deal with his relationship with his mother nor how to express his emotions to her. He was dealing with not having a job or direction for life on top of all the trauma he had already experienced prior to this. He took the stress from all of that out on me.

One day, we were at his mother's house, and she left to go somewhere and left us at the house by ourselves. Another disagreement happened and again, he responded with covert abuse. He went off, broke his dresser, yelled and screamed at me, and then blamed me for it.

The next day, his mother called me asking me what had happened. Even though it was his room, that was her house and she had bought everything in there as well. I told her what happened, and she responded to me saying, "Kayla, you are a beautiful young lady with a good head on your shoulders and a good life ahead of you. Leave my son alone. If he wanted help, he would get it. He is grown and he needs help."

Listening to her say those things killed me because again, I had gotten another sign to not go forward with this relationship. But people didn't know how tired I was of trying and going from one relationship to another and how I seriously didn't want to be alone to feel the pain I had been trying to hide. I started becoming someone I didn't even recognize in the mirror anymore.

After that conversation, I felt like I had to protect him more. I didn't understand how this woman could tell me to leave the man I loved! He needed me! I started to see her as an enemy because she didn't support the false reality I wanted to believe about her son. I made the decision to stop trusting her.

I believed things would get better, but they didn't. Car rides became a nightmare. If things escalated in the car, our lives would be in danger. He would park the car in mid-drive on the road to prove a point, causing danger not only to ourselves but to the people around us. The people who were in the car would always be scared. When the car rides became the place where we were fighting the most, my responses to this trauma went from freezing up to fighting back.

When you go through a traumatic experience, you knowingly or unknowingly respond in four different ways: fight which is responding to any perceived threat; flight which is fleeing or running from the perceived threat; freeze is being unable to move in a situation that is perceived as a threatening situation; then lastly, fawn which is trying to avoid conflict and threatening situations all together by pleasing everyone.

One night, we were in his car with three of my friends, driving back to campus. We started arguing in the car, but I was trying to wait until we got to campus and unloaded the car to respond but I couldn't. I started to respond back to his disrespect in the car and we began arguing. We pulled up to my dorm and before we got out of the car, I threw my cup of water in his face and walked away from the car. He got out, screamed at me, and went out like a gorilla and banged his arms on the car and put a dent in it.

My friends were terrified and didn't want to be around us anymore.

From that moment on, people noticed the chaos in our relationship and called it "fighting."

"You guys have to stop fighting."
"This isn't healthy!"

They didn't realize that I was being abused and I was just responding to my trauma.

That wasn't the only thing that made going to college together complicated.

Before he graduated, the Shapeshifter and I gained a horrible reputation and an unwanted relationship with the authorities and the police.

One night, as the Shapeshifter and I were arguing outside his dorm room, he tried to leave me outside to make a point. He pushed and shoved me up against the cemented staircase that led to the side door in the back of his dormitory and slammed the door.

I stood outside trying to cool down. My roommate came down because I had called her, and I needed someone to help calm me down. I was scratched up and bleeding on my arm and leg.

He then called campus security on me because I had something of his and I had forgotten that I even had it. I was more pissed about that than what he had previously done.

The security came yelling and screaming at me, being extremely aggressive, and telling me to give him the Shapeshifter things and to leave. I was so scared and felt so threatened that I responded back aggressively too. My friend saw that things were going to get ugly and that the police were about to be called so she apologized to the security on my behalf and asked if she could walk with me to calm me down. He said yes. She took my hand and walked me to the dorm. I cried the whole night.

For the next two weeks, the Shapeshifter and I had an open case with our university. We were being investigated because of that incident.

I hated that I was connected to someone who didn't care what our reputation looked like! Still, I tried to cover for him!
Now, we had begun to gain a violent reputation and a bad relationship with security and the police.

As the relationship progressed, I made it a point to try and change things. He was a gifted musician and was called, one day, by the worship leader of a multicultural church who had heard about him. It was like a blessing in disguise. I believed that this was the thing we needed. A new environment. A new church home where we could seek God together. Something needed to change.

The first time we visited the church, it felt like home. As we were evolving and talking about marriage, it felt like the next thing to do was to choose a church of our own.

As we started to consistently go to that new church, many doors began to open for him. He and I gained a community of believers our age who I felt could help us.

I wanted him to move out of his mother's house, find a good job and just marry me. I was ready to fully step into the role I was already playing. He wanted the same thing as me, just not at that moment. I wanted to rush marriage because I felt like it would bring us the stability we needed.

That new church was extremely established. It had been there for years, doing ministry and growing. It was also a big church. It had a main church building, a Spanish church location, a small elementary school, and some houses on its property. The houses on the property were occupied by people who worked for the church.

I started asking questions, hoping there was some way the Shapeshifter could move from his mother's house to live in one of those houses.

I began getting close to one of the worship leaders at the church who was a woman. She was a beautiful, sweet soul. The abuse had gotten worse, and I didn't want to just tell anyone what was going on. I felt like I could trust her with pretty much anything.

As soon as the Shapeshifter and I became a member of the church, we started to get his application together for him to move to the church campus.

That's when I decided to break up with him.

I told him that I couldn't deal with the abuse anymore. He tried so hard to tell me that he was going to change. He promised me that he was going to go to therapy. But he genuinely didn't care about me. He only cared about himself. He just didn't want me to tell anyone what was truly going on and he realized that his "helper" was leaving. I did everything for this man. I carried him through his darkest time and got the backlash for it. I got the shortest end of every stick when I was with him.

I was so tired of feeling powerless in the relationship, so I would break up with him. I had broken up with him many times before, and I did that to feel like I was back in control.
When I would leave the relationship, he would start to act right, giving me the respect I desired. He would get things in place to get counseling or talk to mentors to help him grow but it would only last a couple of weeks or a month.

When we broke up this time, I was a bit determined because I was tired, and I knew I couldn't keep being treated like this.

I still went to the same church and remained a part of the ministries in which I was already involved so we still saw each other and were connected.

That first Sunday after breaking up, I went to lunch with the worship leader that I had started getting close to. She asked me how I was doing, and I told her in the best way that I could that I wasn't okay. She asked me what had happened, and it was like I puked out everything that I had been holding in since the relationship started.

I told her that I left because he kept putting his hands on me.

I felt safe around her. She was a very soft-spoken, meek, and humble spirit who wasn't biased and wasn't going to judge me for staying with my abuser.

By the end of the conversation, I felt affirmed and confident in my decision to walk away.

But in about two more weeks, we were back together.

No one healed. No one sought out help or counsel. No minds were changed. It had just been a break.

We got back together with hopes that things would get better, but reality hit me suddenly when I acknowledged the fact that no work had been done on either one of our parts. I went back to the abusive cycle because I didn't know how to leave for good. This relationship was different, more different than any relationship I had experienced.

Nonetheless, I was tired of everything in this relationship from the abuse to the cycle and I hated the way I was being treated and not being appreciated but I wasn't done though.

The summer going into my senior year quickly approached and things, I thought, had gotten better. Because the Shapeshifter was an alumnus, he was able to still use resources at our college such as free counseling. We were getting counseling together. You would think counseling and that kind of self-accountability would come into play and change things, but it didn't.
 He still didn't have a job and his car had broken down, so I was the only one working and only one who had a vehicle. Things were so tough for no reason. I walked out of the counseling center after our session one day feeling discouraged about my life and relationship. I had started becoming depressed and numb again. Noticing this in my behavior after this session, the Shapeshifter sat me down and asked me what was wrong.

We were at our college, in the hallway, sitting on one of the benches. When I responded by saying "nothing, I'm just tired," he yelled at me, telling me how I was ungrateful and didn't see him trying. He grabbed my hands, wrestled me for my keys, and took them. He walked out the doors to the parking lot, took my car, and left me there.

I called a mutual mentor that we had who worked at our college. I asked him nicely to get in contact with the Shapeshifter, take him home, and to ask him to give me my car back. He agreed.

"What happened, Kayla?" He asked me, confused and a bit irritated.

With tears in my eyes, I responded "he's always angry. He always blames me for everything. I didn't do anything! I show up, I fight for him, and this relationship and I get a nigga who does this! He hurt me and took my car for not responding to his question?!"

The Shapeshifter dropped off my car. I got in it, planning to just cry and go to sleep while the mentor took the Shapeshifter home.

While driving, I started to get pissed thinking of all the times I showed up for him, lied for him, paid and repaired damages he made, took the blame for his actions, and how things were turning out the opposite of how I thought they were going to go so I drove to his place.

Mind you, he had moved into his new place on the church campus but did nothing for the abuse except expose it more.

Neighbors would hear the chaos, screams, fighting, and said or did nothing.

I suffered from the abuse and was reacting to it but because I wasn't educated on abuse culture, I didn't know what reactive abuse was.

Reactive abuse is when someone who is being abused finally responds. It could look like you are both harming and hurting each other equally but it's not.

I arrived at his house, ready to go off! Ready for whatever was next. His front door was locked but I could see him inside, talking to the mentor.

I went to the back door which was always open or easy to open. I opened the back door. There was another door that divided the back of the house from the front, and it was always locked. I went in and began stomping around, picking up and getting the things that I had bought. I had done so much for this man, and I couldn't take it anymore, so I began taking everything that was mine.

He and the mentor came to the back of the house where I was after they heard me ripping clothes off racks and throwing things up on the wall, making noise.

The Shapeshifter charged towards me with all his force and threw me to the ground. We started to wrestle on the ground, but he put all his body weight on me and began choking me.

I was so happy.

I was so happy that someone was finally present to see what he did to me behind closed doors.

Someone saw it and witnessed him and what he did to me. This wasn't all in my head this time!

"What are you doing?!" Our mentor screamed.

The Shapeshifter got off me. I got up and ran to the front of the house, to his room, because I wasn't done. I wanted everything back!

They both ran after me. As soon as I got to his room, he grabbed me, and I slapped his face. He then picked up a chair and threw it at me. It missed me and broke on the wall.

Our mentor tried to intervene, to stop the Shapeshifter, but when he tried, he pushed and threw him across the room.

I ran out of the house, but I didn't leave the area. I sat in my car and waited. I wasn't leaving until I had my things!

I called our mentor and asked him to get my things. He told me that this was crazy, and he was leaving because this was too much for him. I seriously didn't care about anything else but to get revenge.

He told me he was calling the police if I didn't leave. Because we already had a bad history with authorities, I took that as a warning and left.

Tomorrow came and just as if nothing had happened, we were back together.

Nothing got better though I thought they were, because things around us were getting better like being a part of a new church, him having a new home, and him finally getting a job working for me at an after-school program at a local elementary school where I was a supervisor for the YMCA. Nothing about our relationship got better.

The fights continued. I was becoming deeply depressed and suicidal while frequently having panic attacks that came in form of hyperventilation, seizures, or complete shock.

One of our last fights showed me how emotionally numb I had become.

One day during the summer, I came over to his house wanting to talk. I wanted to express to him that I was unhappy. I was coming to talk, open to hearing how I could be making him unhappy as well and hoping to figure out ways we could solve this problem and try to do things right.

As I got to his home, I prayed to start the conversation out right and bring God into it. I hadn't formed a full sentence when he became defensive and stopped listening to everything I was saying altogether.

I told him that I wasn't trying to fight with him or argue. To show him how tired I was of fighting, I told him that we could finish the talk when he was ready.

As I tried to walk out, he took my phone and keys and locked me outside his house.

Again, I was so depleted and over everything. I didn't have the energy to fight anymore so I knocked on the back door which had a glass window. I knocked on the window. No screaming, no fighting, nothing. Just knocking.

The glass shattered on my hand, slicing my hand in three different spots. Blood was gushing out and spilling on the deck outside his house, but I didn't feel anything. I kept knocking.

He came and saw blood everywhere, grabbed my wounded hand, took me to the bathroom, and ran cold water. He then shoved my wounded hand aggressively under the water to clean it. I was so numb that I still didn't say a word. He wrapped my hand in bandages and as I tried to walk out, he locked us in the bathroom. The bathroom door surprisingly locked from the outside instead of from the inside so the only way we could get out was if someone from the outside let us out.

As he locked us in, he pushed and pinned me to the wall. I blacked out as he started yelling at me, pushing me back and forth, while my back and the back of my head fiercely hit the wall.

He ripped my clothes off my body, and we fell to the ground. As he screams at me and begins hitting me. I still didn't move or say a word.

After he finished having his blow-up, he finally calmed down. He took off his shirt and gave it to me to cover my naked body. He called his friend to come and let us out. Before his friend opened the door, the Shapeshifter grabbed me saying, "don't leave me."

A few weeks passed, and I went to my mother's house. My mother began noticing the huge shift in my personality. I looked so defeated. She looked at me and asked, "why are you settling?"

I looked at her, confused.

"What?" I responded.

"Why are you settling?"

I was so confused and angry at her for asking me this!

"How dare you? You, out of all people? The person who got me in this situation?! The woman who got involved with a deadbeat who left me and my sisters and never loved us?! And you question me on how I cope with my pain?? Fuck you!"

"Some people don't get that happily ever after. Some don't get that love and the man of their dreams. I'm one of those people and I'm okay with that," I said to her.

I ended the conversation by telling her never to say anything like that to me again and I left.

Senior year was quickly approaching for me, and I was so exhausted. I wanted things to change so badly.

My first week of school approached and I had to get prepared for my kids' performance. I had a mime ministry for kids in the second and third grades. They were dancing to "Free" by KiKi Sheard on Saturday, September 2nd, 2018, at a women's banquet.

For three days straight, Monday, Tuesday and Wednesday, I was attacked in my sleep. I was being spiritually attacked and each dream was different. I didn't tell anyone, but I felt like God was warning me. That Wednesday, I wrote the Shapeshifter a letter and told him how much I loved him and wanted to make this work. I told him in the letter that if he was willing to, we could start counseling again, and do the work to be healthy.

Though we were together all the time, we did not live together. My scholarship required me to live in the dorms on campus or in college housing. The Shapeshifter lived in his own home, on the church campus still.

He didn't come over that Wednesday or want to talk. He said he was tired, and we could talk at lunch the next day in my college's dining hall.

Again, we worked together at the local school, at the after-school program. I was the supervisor, and he was a paraprofessional. Around that time, his car was repossessed, and we were using my car. He had my car most of the time, so when he arrived on Thursday, he came with my car.

I felt a shift happening in my life and I knew that God was doing something in me that year since it was my last year of college. Many of us who feel this type of awakening want to bring people with us who just don't want to go.

He arrived for lunch on Thursday, and we talked. Though he didn't blow up, he seemed extremely uninterested and unmoved. It seemed like he didn't care about anything I had to say or what had been going on with me. I was so frustrated and over everything that was going on, so I decided to just end the conversation. For some reason, on that day, I couldn't tolerate him and his actions. He was so disrespectful and disgustingly rude!

We walked out of the dining hall and got on the elevator. We began to argue and exchange words in the elevator and decided that it was over.

We got off and went our separate ways. I realized that he still had my car and keys and demanded it back. He left before I knew it and I texted him. "I wish you would die."

He didn't respond and hours passed.

I walked into my Geology class and a girl who sat behind me asked if I had seen the Shapeshifter's posts on Facebook.

"No, what did it say?"

She told me that he uploaded a screenshot of someone saying they wished he would die but he dropped out the person's name.

As I scrolled down on the post, I saw so many people commenting and saying many things in his defense.

I was heated!

 "How could he do something like this to me? The one who had been protecting him this whole time!"

He didn't respond or talk to me the rest of Thursday and Friday.

Friday after class, I called my mother and grandmother to go get my car from him. I asked Papo to pick me up from school so I could get to my car.

I got home, got in my car, and drove over to his house. He wasn't there.

I went in through the back of the house, still angry. I poured detergent everywhere, destroying things, and left before he got there because my kids were performing the next morning and I had to be in right mindset for them.

I tried texting and calling people we were connected to, asking them to get in contact with him so we could talk. I told any and everyone what was going on, out of fear.

I knew that it was over.

Saturday, September 2nd came, and I was so speechless at how everything had changed between the Shapeshifter and me. I was so codependent on this person that it was like someone took crack away from a crackhead. I was losing my mind.

My kids danced to "Free" by Kiki Sheard and did amazing. This was our last performance for a while because I had to focus on school and graduating since it was my senior year, but I couldn't focus or be present at the banquet because I was thinking about the Shapeshifter, hoping we could work things out and be together.

Still, I hadn't received a response from him so once the women's banquet was over, I dropped some kids off and headed over to his house again.

I was calm that day and genuinely wanted to talk and ask why he was doing this to me.

I was confused on why a couple of words did this to him and made him want to leave but he had been beating my ass the whole relationship and I stayed? It wasn't fair to me.

On Saturdays, he would play the drums for our Spanish church service, so I knew that he was either there, at the church practicing, or about to be.

I drove over and knocked on the door. No one answered.

I went through the back door and sat at the back of the house and waited. I even fell asleep and later noticed that a few hours had passed.

I woke up and noticed that he had left to go to the Spanish church to practice. Service usually started at 6:30 pm and rehearsal was an hour before that.

I tried to go and open the door that divided the front of the house from the back and when I realized that I couldn't open it, I slid down with my back on the wall and began to cry.

"How can this be happening?" I thought to myself, confused and honestly tired.

As a matter of fact, I was done. I was so done with everything: the relationship, the Shapeshifter, my life, everything!

As I was reflecting, two leaders from the church came in, both white, a man and a woman.

"Kayla?" they asked.

I was so scared, so I didn't answer. They looked around for a bit. I could have tried to hide but I was done. They finally found me. They both jerked back, startled, because of how I looked. I can't even imagine how I must I've looked to them.

They asked me to come out and I told them to give me a second.

I finally came out and they told me that the Shapeshifter said that I had been harassing him for the past couple of days and that I needed to leave the church campus.

I just stood there.

"How could they say this to me? If they only knew what I had been putting up with for almost two years, they would put this man behind bars!" I thought to myself.

But I was a black woman who knew that her role as a black woman was to protect black men.

I knew that if I took the Shapeshifter to jail, he wouldn't get the help he needed so I put up with it. I put up with everything.

I listened to them and walked away.

I got into my car and drove to the Spanish church to find the Shapeshifter.

I got there with tears rolling down my face and went to find him. I was done!

I walked into the sanctuary, and he walked out as soon as he saw me. This was the first time in this whole relationship that I completely snapped!

We walked outside the sanctuary, and he asked me why I was there? He told me to go home.

At that exact moment, I blacked out.

I started swinging on him, pushing him, doing everything I should have done before today. People started noticing and walked out of the sanctuary to stop me.

"YOU LIAR!" I kept screaming and crying.

A girl held me back and as he ran off, I fell to the ground, crying.

No one offered to hear my side. No one asked me if I was okay. No one asked me what I needed. No one took me inside of their house to make me feel safe. No one saw my pain. They told me to leave. In the mental state that I was in, the church told me to leave. They banned me from the church and told me to leave.

I sat in my car, which was parked outside the Spanish church, and cried. I screamed and cried for 10 minutes straight, hoping someone would come out there and see my pain and hug me.

After 10 minutes, I decided that I was done with life and that I was going to die.

I made the decision to commit suicide that day. I didn't want to feel my death; I wanted it to be quick and final.

I had two plans:

Plan 1. To back my car up far enough and, with high speed, crash into the Spanish church building.

Plan 2. I was going to cause a car accident on the road that the church was on.

I chose plan 2.

I started driving, in my mentally unstable headspace, and I got behind a blue truck. I decided that the blue truck would be the car that was going to help me end my life.

As I sped up behind the truck, about to crash, I swerved off the road.

I had seen a little girl in the back of the truck.

I said to God, "I want to hurt me, just me, not anyone else."

He showed me at that moment that killing myself was going to not only hurt other people but that it would kill them as well, figuratively and literally.

I didn't tell God that I was going to live. I was just willing to wait a bit.

I continued driving but I was screaming and crying the whole time and got to a point where I couldn't see or breathe.

I ended up slowing down in a neighborhood I had never seen before and found a spot to park my car and just sit.

"God, I'm tired," I said.

"Your people have hurt me! Why did they do this to me?! I HATE THEM!" I screamed as I cried.

I wrote and sent my mother, sisters, mentor, and father a suicide letter and turned off my phone.

As I sent it, I was determined to slit my throat in the car with a tool or whatever object I could find in there. But before I could, I suddenly became very sleepy and fell asleep.

As I was sleeping, I heard God say, "get up, get up. I have so much for you to do. You must speak for those who can't speak for themselves. Get up."

"What?! Did you not see what I just went through?!" I asked God.

He said, "I know! Get up! I have so much for you to do! I will restore everything back to you. I will restore the years the swarming locusts stole from you! Everything, even the husband that I promised you. Trust me and let everything go! Give it to me. It's not your time. I need you to live!"

I chose to trust God and that night; I was taken to the hospital thinking I was going to be admitted to the psych ward because I was still suicidal. They didn't admit me, but they kept me in the hospital for a couple of hours.

My friends who took me to the hospital dropped me off around 2 am.

I couldn't sleep so I stayed up all night and day, processing what had just happened to me. Even though God told me to let the Shapeshifter go, I didn't want to. I wasn't ready to.

And even though I chose to live, I was still rebellious towards God.

I told God that I didn't want to be appealing to men anymore and I didn't want to be married. I told him that I was going to be single for the rest of my life.

To prove how serious I was, I shaved my hair off the very next day.

I hated myself. I hated being a woman. I hated being a black woman. I hated that this whole time I protected a man who not once ever protected me.

I hated everything about life, but life didn't care. Life still went on. I had to go to school the next day and I still had to go to work.

I learned to just cope with it by allowing myself to feel the desire to die but choosing to live and doing whatever I needed to do to stay alive.

If you thought that it was over, it wasn't.

I continuously reached out to the Shapeshifter every chance I got, expressing to him everything I felt until he blocked me. And even after he blocked me, I would still create numbers and accounts to reach out to him.

I wasn't ready for the truth to be exposed about my relationship. I wasn't ready for people to try to give me sympathy. I wasn't ready to feel uncomfortable when people expressed that they felt bad for me. I didn't want anyone's sympathy! I wanted people to leave me alone and I wanted the Shapeshifter back to fill my void!

But things never go the way you want them to, especially when God is in it.

The end of October came, and I finally came to the realization that maybe he wasn't going to come back. The mutual mentor we had reached out to me. He wanted to check in on me to see how I was doing but he also said he needed to tell me something.

We met outside the coffee shop on my university's campus. It was a nice, warm night and physically I looked okay, but mentally you could notice when I talked, that I still wasn't functional nor stable. We began talking and I was anxiously waiting for him to tell me what he wanted to tell me.

In my mind, I thought he was going to tell me that the Shapeshifter had a new girlfriend or something like that and honestly, I was prepared for it.

But no, he told me that the Shapeshifter's mother had paid for a restraining order to be put out against me and that they were taking me to court.

"What the fuck? But why?"

"I don't know," he said.

I got up without ending the conversation and walked inside the coffee shop to try and make it into the bathroom before I broke down crying. I threw the drink I had in my hand down before running into the bathroom with tears streaming down my face.

Two of my friends came in and tried to comfort me but I couldn't talk. I didn't want to.

I walked out the door to clean up the mess I had made when I threw the drink, but a friend of mine was already cleaning it up for me.

The cafe was connected to one of the university's halls, where we had our classes, so I walked to one of the classrooms and my two friends followed me. I didn't stay anything.

I started writing on the dry erase board with a marker...

"God loves me

God is with me

God had never left me

God will never leave me

God sees me

God loves me

God will forever be my King

God will heal me

God will fight for me"

My friends walked into the room and saw me writing. I finally told them what had happened, and they also started crying for me. They hugged me and prayed for me.

That whole night, I cried.

I got served my restraining order papers at the post office and my court date was set for November 9th.

I had two options: show up, defend my name and try to win, or don't show up and take whatever order they put out against me.

I chose to show up for myself.

At that moment, I didn't make the decision to only show up for me court-wise. I was going to show up for myself, literally.

I realized how far off I had gotten in life. I forgot about the mentoring group Gladiolus, the angels God sent me to help me make better decisions in life, and my spiritual father. I felt like once again, I had lost my way.

But that was a lie. I had never truly committed to living for God.
I realized that I had been committed to ministries, programs, churches, and organizations but never to Jesus Himself.

I knew that I had to start doing some hard work to get reconnected to my support systems and to heal. I didn't want to live the same way anymore, so I repented to God and was ready to really face myself. I knew this journey was going to be long, but I also knew it was going to be worth it.

I needed to prepare for my promise!

Step 1 to restoration journey:
I went back to counseling.
I wanted the same counselor that I had before while I was in my abusive relationship, but her caseload was full of other clients. She was a blonde-haired, blue-eyed white woman who was as sweet as pie. After a few sessions filled with me expressing my pain from being fatherless, she introduced me to a book called "Longing for Daddy: Healing from the pain of an absent or emotionally distant father" by Monique Robinson.

It was a regular reader but also a workbook. During most of our sessions, we worked through this book but didn't go past chapter 2.

I realized that God wanted me to finish the book on my own, so I bought the book for myself and started reading it again.

Step 2.
My new therapist gave me the strategy of writing how I felt in a journal daily. She explained to me that this was one of the healthiest things a person could do to express what they felt.

So I bought a journal and began journaling in it, but I also printed out a monthly blank calendar to write my emotions. Emotionally, I was all over the place and most times, unavailable. My heart and mind were disconnected, and I deeply desired for everything on the inside of me to be in one accord.

Step 3.
I stayed connected with my support system. I met with people who loved me and cared for me deeply and who wanted to love me back to life. I hung out with friends and people who were safe places for me. I talked to mentors, spiritual leaders, and professors who gave me direction. I met with those people on a regular basis, if not weekly, bi-weekly.

Step 4.
I watched sermons and Christian videos that helped me seek God for the first time.

I began to be inspired by a woman named Jackie Hill Perry. Her courage to tell her testimony changed my life. She was recorded in an interview explaining different ways to start a relationship with God.

She simply broke down the Scripture where Jesus says, "if you loved me, you would keep my commandments."

She followed up by saying, "how can you love someone you don't know? Or trust someone that you don't know with your life? To love someone is to know someone."
She said that she studied the Gospels to learn Jesus and then she learned to love Him, trust Him and obey His commandments.

I was so moved and amazed by that interview that I did just that. I began reading the Gospels Starting with Mark.

Step 5.
I started getting my life in order and putting myself on a strict schedule. Alongside the journal, I bought a planner too where I marked out what I had to do each day. In my planner, I would schedule a time to journal, read my Word, go to work, go to class, meet with overseers, and do other things that were going to help me show up for myself.

Step 6.
To motivate me and keep my mind determined, I created a wall in my dorm room where I put pictures, quotes, Scriptures, statements, goals, the promises God gave me, and aspirations that reminded me every day to choose to live.

Step 7.
I prayed daily. I started the process of breaking soul ties and trauma bonds with the men I had been with and stopped fornicating.

I began doing the work. I began healing! I began to come alive! This was the hardest work I had ever done but it was worth it.

The week of my court date was right around the corner, but I wasn't worried. I was calm. I was showing up for myself and doing my part. I just knew God was going to show up for me.

The day came and I arrived in court. I saw my ex-boyfriend's mother and then I saw him with three other people who turned out to be his lawyer and witnesses.

I came with two male mentors.

We got into the courtroom and the judge was a white woman. The Shapeshifter explained that he wanted a restraining order to put out against me for 3 years because he was fearful that I was going to kill him. He told the judge that he was afraid to sleep at night because he thought I was going to come and kill him in his sleep.

In my mind, I thought two things:
1. I wanted to ask the Shapeshifter why he thought I wanted to kill him and what could have caused me to feel that way?
2. Secondly, I wanted to tell him that it was probably God putting fear in his heart for the things he had done to me and lied about.

I represented and defended myself and to be honest, I did one hell of a job even with his witnesses coming to the stand to testify against me and a lot of push back from the lawyer.

Nonetheless, that wasn't enough.

The Shapeshifter won the case and the court agreed to a one-year restraining order.

I couldn't believe it.

"How can this possibly happen? I was doing the work. I was being obedient!" It was yet another slap in my face.

That night, I didn't cry. I was pissed.

"How could he win?" I thought.

 The Scripture that explained my emotions at that point was Psalms 13:1-4

"How long, Lord? Will you forget me forever? How long will you hide your face from me? How long must I wrestle with my thoughts and day after day have sorrow in my heart? How long will my enemy triumph over me? Look on me and answer, Lord my God. Give light to my eyes, or I will sleep in death, and my enemy will say, "I have overcome him," and my foes will rejoice when I fall."

I was more than devastated. I was destroyed.

For the next 3 nights, I couldn't sleep without the Bible audio or Christian/gospel music being played.

Spiritual warfare became evident like never before in my life. I got night terrors and threats from people who knew my ex-boyfriend and never got to hear my side of the story.

Church leaders contacted me but not one of them wanted to hear my side. They shunned me and banished me and counted me out. They took his side only because he had money to paint a false picture in the courtroom. He was only able to lie because I covered for him ever since the relationship started!

I protected him. But when it was time to protect me, he chose to protect himself.

Nonetheless, I decided to push through my pain and continued my journey to show up for myself. I will graduate and form a great relationship with God.

I was blessed to finish my first semester and started to see God turn things around in my favor. I was offered another job at my school and God started to use me as a leader in different places and groups, representing the university. I didn't want to do anything else but to be God's mouthpiece.

As I continued my journey with myself, my support system, and God, I began getting the courage to ask God to do big things in my life. I wanted God to use me.

The book I was reading titled Longing for Daddy, was the leading thing that validated me for the first time in my life, it showed me why I was the way I was and why I did the things I did. It gave me the understanding I so desperately longed for, and it taught me the things I needed to go into my next season.

1. It confirmed that my low self-esteem, no self-worth, bitterness, people-pleasing with no boundaries, and need to overcompensate were a direct result of being fatherless.

2. I also realized that part of my reason for being controlling and a perfectionist, who kept things in order externally, was to fool myself and others from my unresolved issues. I also gravitated towards men who needed fixing; projects to work on, for the same reason: so they couldn't see my issues.

3. I realized by reading this book that I became an overachiever to fill the void of having no self-worth, low self-esteem, and no value.

4. I found it difficult to give God control over my life due to my fatherlessness.

5. The book gave me hope that I could change by educating me through the workbook, Scripture, prayer, and by giving me ideas to work on and evaluate.

6. I realized how aimless my life was and that I had no sense of direction because of how deep this Daddy wound was.

7. The author stated that having an absent or emotionally distant father is traumatic and that fatherless children have been traumatized. I accepted this was traumatic.

8. The author gave charts and facts that educated me on the effects of this trauma at every stage of life. I saw how a fatherless child would respond and act out, which

helped me understand that I was never a "Tasmanian Devil." I was fatherless.

9. She stated that she would change us, the readers', belief system and reestablish God as our Father.

10. The author gave the reason why fathers leave. I, for the first time in my life, saw my father as a human being. She explained that in the same way the fall of man affected us, it affected our fathers and that the enemy sets out to attack, kill and destroy our fathers just as he sets out to do the same to the rest of us. The author stated, "you are engaged in a spiritual war, not a father-daughter battle."

11. The book helped me see myself and my father in a new light which gave me understanding and validation. Then, it gave direction on what to pray about, study on, and bring to my advisors and counselor to unpack and work through more.

12. The author affirmed, saw my brokenness, need for a father but then held me accountable which was the pruning process. It was cutting off dead things in me like habits, mindsets, and behaviors that came from not having a dad. God, being our Father, must hold us accountable to act and walk like Jesus by doing things such as

examining ourselves, creating boundaries, stopping procrastination, being lazy, and reading our Bible.

13. She brought up things in the book that were hard to talk about but needed to be addressed. After redeeming God's place as a Father, she laid out what true love was. (1 Corinthians 13: 1-8.)

14. The author also acknowledged in the book that being fatherless opens a child up to being abused or being put in abusive situations. She stated that it was more likely for fatherless children to be abused and/or grow up to be in abusive relationships. This was the piece of information that allowed me to start forgiving myself and then go forth in the direction of understanding and acceptance with myself.

15. Next, came the hard part. The author has a chapter in there called "A Man Like Dad" where she states that the men, we are pursuing have no fruit like our fathers. I was so afraid to read this chapter, but I needed to read it the most. I needed it. I needed direction on what a man looked like which was nowhere near the guys I even twitched my eye at. This chapter showed me that man God has for me and what qualities he should have. Not perfection but pursuit.

16. The last chapters fully redeemed me and made me a Daddy's girl. It explained that God is Yahweh- Rapha, God of healing and restoration.

The only thing I felt like she missed was acknowledging that at times, some children or adults who were abused or witnessed abuse, most likely become abusers without knowing. I studied this book and I studied. I gained so much insight, education, and understanding. Reading this book also gave me the healing and direction I didn't know I needed.

After this, I had a desire to tell people about what I had learned so they could learn too.

I prayed and asked God to allow me to tell my story, preach and teach people the things I had learned in this season! The desire to tell people where I had been increased in me.

I wasn't ready to be open about being abused yet, but I started wanting to break the stigma on therapy and mental and emotional awareness because these subjects were still taboo.

Because of the trauma I had suffered from dating someone who was mentally ill and was never treated, along with having my own illness, issues, and unprocessed baggage, I got this deep burden to educate people on suicide and mental health around that time.

At the end of my senior year, God gave me the opportunity to preach for the first time at my college. I was one of the only black women who preached at my predominantly white institution.

I was ready to give the world a glimpse of what I knew God wanted to do in my life.

I was asked to preach by the "Family" team at my school which was a board of students who facilitated when other students sang and preached on our campus.

To me, it felt like it was finally my time, though it wasn't. It was just the beginning, and I hadn't even scratched the surface of where God wanted to take me, how He wanted to fully use me, or who He wanted me to speak for.

I only thought it was for people with mental challenges and people who survived suicide attempts but God told me more! He wanted to do more. He was going to use me differently in every season of my life.

Wednesday night came and I was ready to preach the word that God had given to me to preach.

My family and friends came out to support me and I was ready but also nervous like never before.

I was so nervous but honey, once I hit that podium, I felt like I was finally in my rightful place: before God's people and being God's mouthpiece. The chapel was packed from downstairs to the balcony.

The title of my message was "What Are You Still a Slave To?"

The Scripture I used to be Exodus 3:1-10.

God had revealed Himself to Moses through the burning bush. He came to Moses because of the cries of the Israelites. God called Moses' name saying "Moses, Moses" and Moses responded saying, "Here I am."

Moses saying "here I am" was a place of trust and obedience to God. That was the place I felt God pushing me to be but also the message He wanted me to deliver to His people that night.

My purpose was to identify to the people of God what they were slaves to, acknowledge what was keeping them from fully trusting God, and help them start the process of reconciling themselves back to God so they could be in full submission to Him and be used for His perfect purpose.

I started off with a quote from Harriet Tubman followed by two questions.

"I have freed a thousand slaves, and I could have freed a thousand more only if they knew they were slaves.".

I opened with this quote because most of the time, we don't know that we are slaves to things or know when someone has us in bondage.

I then gave the back story of Moses and what brought him to the place of saying "here I am" to God. I explained that Moses was just like me. He had faults and flaws and even pushed back when God first called him to deliver the people of Israel.

Follow-up question 1: "What are you slave to?"

Follow-up question 2: "What needs to be done for you to be free?"

The Holy Spirit was very strong in the chapel and many people were moved by the analogy in my message. So many of these people had been hurting and in bondage and for most of them, it was their first time acknowledging that out loud.

I ended it by telling my story and what I was a slave to.

I was transparent and told them that I had become my own worst enemy because of my own disobedience to God. I was committed to doing things my own way. I told a part of my story for the first time. I talked about how I attempted to kill myself and that if anyone in the room needed help that night, they should seek help such as therapy and support.

I closed by telling the people that we have a duty to be like Moses and say "here I am" to God and be used for His purpose.

We ended with an activity. We had a wooden cross and I put it in the front of the stage. The activity was to write down, on a piece of paper that I had put under everyone's chair with a small pencil, what they were a slave to and throw it down at the cross.

As people did that, the song "Deliver Me" by LeAndria Johnson was playing to end the night off.

Chains were broken that night, not only off the people in the room but off me as well. I was stepping into what I knew God had called me to be and doing what He was calling me to do.

PART TWO: THE JOURNEY TO THE PROMISE

"Simon, Simon, Satan has asked to sift all of you as wheat. But I have prayed for you, Simon, that your faith may not fail. And when you have turned back, strengthen your brothers."

Luke 22:31-32 NIV

THE PREDATOR

Eager and ready to do God's will was an understatement and I didn't care what that would look like. After God delivered me, and set me free, He started using me. In my last year of college, I started to share my testimony more, got more involved on my campus, and led a women's group called L.I.F.T (Ladies in Faith Together). I was blessed and honored to be in leadership and work in spaces that brought change to my school.

I was a founding member of groups that brought awareness of diversity and inclusion to my college. The Lord also allowed me to graduate that year even though I was failing two classes in my major. He equipped me to do His work with the love and support of lifelong friends, family, professors, mentors, and spiritual leaders. My relationship with my family began to get restored. I started setting healthy boundaries with not only friends but with family as well. I also started letting go of the past hurt and pain. My father was the first on my list to forgive, and then my mother. My relationship with my sisters was eventually restored as well.

After graduating college, I was led to take an internship job in Louisville, Kentucky. This new job blessed me with my first home church, new friends, and a set of mentors. It gave me the foundation I needed as a believer and to live a healthy life. It taught me the importance of the Sabbath, the day of rest for believers. My relationship with God flourished! Everywhere I went to serve in ministry, people could see the evidence of God moving in my life.

God was healing me. He was restoring everything that I had lost, except a romantic relationship.

It was as if everything God had done and was doing wasn't enough for me or complete without a romantic relationship.

But God continued using my experiences to influence different workplaces and communities in Kentucky.

I was admired by many people because of my heart for God, diligence in my journey, and transparency with my story. For this reason, I was asked to speak on many platforms between Ohio and Kentucky.

I still wasn't satisfied though.

A year later, I felt the push to entrepreneurship. I became a certified life coach because of how secure I felt in myself, what God had taught me and how He had turned me around. I also had the desire to bring awareness to mental health and emotional intelligence, especially for the black community. During this time, I was a part of a multicultural nondenominational church, and I was serving, but I felt like I was still missing something.

I was growing quickly. After a year of being a part of that church and getting the passion to start a business, I finally did it. I started the business.

The Talitha Koum Experience was birthed. "Talitha Koum" is Aramaic and means "Little girl, arise".

My business purpose would be to give people a shifting experience. The organization would provide life coaching, tools, and resources so people can gain knowledge and become aware of themselves emotionally, mentally, and spiritually. Anyone who would use these services will redeem their identity, be empowered to embrace who they are, and be released into their purpose.

While doing this business, I felt the pull to truly reconnect to the black community with the voice and business I now had. I also felt the need to connect to the church as well. I quickly got clarity from God concerning this and began transitioning in every aspect of my life: business, church, job, and home.

But again, I was not completely satisfied because God had not fulfilled all the things, He promised me. I felt fulfilled when I was being elevated at first. But not for long.

God told me that He had someone for me! So why was it taking so long?

I was ashamed to say that sometimes, I didn't care about the blessings, and the opportunities to speak on podcasts or the success in the business. All that was on my mind was to love someone and be loved by someone. I started to feel like God was lying to me.

Eventually I started attending a black church in Kentucky. It had been about 6 years since I'd been to a black church but the call to go back was so great. One of the main differences between some multicultural, contemporary churches and some black churches is the emphasis that the black churches put on the power and authority that the believer receives from the Holy Ghost after being baptized in Jesus' name. I had been to many churches across the spectrum and longed for that!

I didn't know what God was about to give me as I stepped foot in this new church. But I was ready. It was a small church on the west side of Louisville, and you could feel the power of God before you even walked through the doors. I was invited by a friend, who was a member named Rachel. I was a part of Rachel's business team and she had invited the whole team to come visit her church.

It had been about three years since I was in a romantic relationship and since I received my deliverance from fornication. There were no "talking stages", no interests, nothing. A cycle started. I would meet a guy, then start believing and being hopeful that God was going to do what He had said, then getting tired of waiting and wanting to see the physical manifestations of His promise to me. Then nothing happened. Even though I was still being used by God on the outside, there was also the reality of a struggle inside of me.

The church I was going to have a similar atmosphere to the church I grew up in. I remembered being in the sanctuary at church as a kid and watching everyone else get what they needed from God. Again, I wanted what everyone else seemed to have had.

My business, career, and friendships were thriving before, but they thrived differently since I started attending this church. The church was Holy Spirit-filled, and the culture of this church was different from what I had ever experienced. I grew up in a black church and been to black churches, but they didn't have power. It wasn't as Holy Spirit-filled as this one. The Pastor was a Prophet, and he was so unique and different from any other leader I had ever had. He was teaching me new things that I had never thought of before such as having power and authority in Jesus' name. Through prayer, fasting, and being around like-minded people, God began showing me signs and wonders related to where I was going next in my life. No one in church, let alone the house I grew up in, spoke in tongues, and we never talked about the Holy Spirit.

My relationship with God started to get to different levels that I had never experienced before, and I knew I needed more of Him.

I desired to step into the totality of who I was created to be as a woman called to do many great things in the kingdom of God. While serving and being a member of this church, I started blooming into this woman of God that I was proud of and wanted to be. In order to go deeper in my walk with God, I knew I needed to receive the Holy Spirit. I wanted the power and authority that everyone around me had but I was afraid. I had always had an image in my mind of what that looked like, and it scared me. I hated feeling out of control of my body and I had the idea that it was going to hurt or that I would lose my mind; nonetheless, I continued deeply longing for it.

Bible studies were on Tuesdays, and I attended faithfully. To everyone else, it seemed as if I had arrived at a good place in life. I finished college, wasn't drowning in debt, had a job, didn't have kids, lived on my own, had a business and I was speaking in different places, telling parts of my story. But my reality was that I was still hurting from many things. In my eyes, I was failing in friendships and relationships. Every time I expected to be settled at a job, with a friend group, church, or a potential relationship, it was like God would move me somewhere else. I just wanted to get to the finish line. I was so unhappy and still felt bound behind closed doors and no one noticed.

On this specific Tuesday night at Bible study, before I walked into the building, I sat in my car feeling so emotionally heavy. A friend of mine had said something to me prior to coming to the Bible study that shook me.

She had observed that when I talked about where I had been and the abuse I had suffered in my last relationship, it was like I only said as much. It was like a filtered version.

That stuck with me as I left her house and as I drove all the way to church for Bible study.

"Why?" I asked myself. "Why do I feel so constrained when I talk about my abuse?"

I had talked about it a lot and I didn't mind telling people, but she was right. I only went so far. I reflected on this as I was sitting in my car.

I gathered the courage and strength to walk into the building and like I always did, I sat in the front, on the right side. I began to weep from the beginning of the first song that our worship leader sang, all the way to when our Pastor walked up to the pulpit. I wept the whole time. I started crying so loud that I removed myself and went to the bathroom.

I hurried into the bathroom of the church, closed the door behind me, fell on my knees and wept like there was not tomorrow. I desperately wanted someone to come in and rescue me, someone to hug me and just hold me. God spoke to me right away. I cried and I cried until the words finally came flying out of my mouth with a huge release.

"I've been so abused! I've been so abused! I've been so hurt! I've been so mistreated! I've been so abandoned!"

My shoulders and chest collapse with a great exhale. It was the first time in almost 3 years that I had allowed myself to feel and admit the things that brought me so much pain. I had started the work to overcome it, but I had never admitted it. I had experienced so much in my life, even before the abuse in my last relationship but at that moment I finally felt safe enough to allow myself to experience the emotions, to acknowledge what had happened, and to release it. I said to myself, "yesterday was the last night I would go to sleep with that burden on me. Tonight I won't leave this place until I am free."

I walked out of that bathroom ready to do whatever it took to get that burden off me. I was ready for war.

I came back out to the sanctuary just in time for prayer. I felt so pushed that I almost ran to the altar ready to receive whatever God had for me. As I walked up to the Pastor, ready to receive a release from him through prayer, he did something different. He spoke to me and spoke
"I release a portion of my anointing into your mouth" and he released me and went on to the next person.

I was confused. I thought he was going to release me by praying for me, but instead, he gave me a portion of his anointing.

"What does that even mean?" I thought to myself.

At that moment I felt a rushing wind, which I knew to be the wind of the Holy Ghost, take over my whole body. I began to weep all over again and fell to the ground, speaking in a language that I had never spoken before. Then I heard God say, "you have the power to release it off of yourself."

I put my hand on my chest speaking in my heavenly language and in English saying, "release it, release it, release it."

That night ended with me feeling a peace and a weight off me like never before.

Even though I had that experience, I needed knowledge!

"What happened to me that night?" I needed to understand.

The following week the Pastor and I met at the church, in his office one day during the week. I came into that meeting with a long list of questions that I had ready to challenge him with concerning my own speculations on the denomination. I didn't understand why we as a church functioned a certain way and what exactly had happened to me last Tuesday at Bible study. Overall, I had a true desire to understand.

He responded with a little shock and laughter. "We are nondenominational but follow the apostolic doctrine."

"What does that mean? I've heard that so many times, "Apostolic doctrine." Can you explain that to me, please?" I asked, ready to finally get an answer.

He asked me to open the Bible to Acts chapter 2 starting at verse 37 and finishing at 47.

"When the people heard this, they were cut to the heart and said to Peter and the other apostles, "Brothers, what shall we do?"

Peter replied, Repent and be baptized, every one of you, in the name of Jesus Christ for the forgiveness of your sins. And you will receive the gift of the Holy Spirit. The promise is for you and your children and for all who are far off—for all whom the Lord our God will call.

With many other words, he warned them; and he pleaded with them, "Save yourselves from this corrupt generation." Those who accepted his message were baptized, and about three thousand were added to their number that day.

Then those who gladly received his word were baptized, and that day of about three thousand souls were added *to them.* And they continued steadfastly in the apostles' doctrine and fellowship, in the breaking of bread, and in prayers. Then fear came upon every soul, and many wonders and signs were done through the apostles. Now all who believed were together, and had all things in common, and sold their possessions and goods, and divided them among all, as anyone had needed.

So continuing daily with one accord in the temple, and breaking bread from house to house, they ate their food with gladness and simplicity of heart, praising God and having favor with all the people. And the Lord added to the church daily those who were being saved."

I had never in my life heard or read that Scripture until now, and I had been baptized twice by that time. No one had ever told me about this Scripture. I had never heard the Gospel like this, and I was extremely overwhelmed and convinced that what I had doubted or thought to be false because of my own experiences, was true. I now knew that all my doubt was because of my own ignorance.

So overwhelmed, I began to cry and reread the Scriptures. I didn't know that the apostolic doctrine was true. If I had not heard this truth that day, I could have died the next day, never having experienced truth, power, and freedom in this lifetime.

My Pastor then told me a story of when he first started pastoring at a Baptist church. He said they had their own ways of doing ministry and they had never heard this Scripture either. One day, he read and preached the Gospel to the congregation from this chapter and after he finished preaching, there was a deep silence. One lady raised her hand and said that she had never heard of baptism, nor had she ever heard the Gospel preached like that in her life. She wanted to be baptized in Jesus' name.

"I do too!" I said, interrupting his story.

I needed to be baptized the right way, now that I knew more. Excited for my next step he prayed for me, hugged me and then we started discussing my baptism date.

I had finally reached a place where I knew I needed to be with God. But just like that, the Predator sniffed me out.

When I first entered the entrepreneurship world, I was blessed and amazed to see so many people like myself, who had chosen to have the courage to step out and walk in their purpose. I had gotten close to one woman in particular who I connected with because we had both suffered domestic violence. We both had many similar experiences in life and that drew us to each other. Since we were moving in the same direction, we tried to use our platforms to promote our individual message and vision but together. We encouraged and lifted each other up.

As I became all that I believed I was always supposed to be, flourishing in all aspects in life, getting connected to like-minded people going in the same direction as me with the same values, getting closer to God in new ways, I finally started feeling complete. I knew that I had to be close to the fulfillment of God's promise of bringing me my husband because all the doors that were opening for me had to be ordained by God.

I didn't know that I was blind then and the enemy noticed and decided that it was time to throw me far from God.

My friend called me one day, telling me about a man she had talked to who had a huge platform and who wanted her to speak on his Christian podcast, which was in another city. She had agreed to do it but only if I was with her. He was okay with that and so she asked me if I would go with her to be on his podcast!

My heart was so warm, and I was full of gratitude!

"You thought of me?" I said to her.

She laughed and said, "yes girl! We must get ready. He wants us there in like two weeks!"

"Perfect." I said, because it gave us enough time to prepare and enough time to get back in town for my baptism.

I had committed to the date of July 4th for my baptism, and I didn't want anything to change or interfere with it because I was so ready to get in that water and be filled with Jesus. I also needed to do this because, on top of many other things, I was the first in my family to be baptized in Jesus' name. I wasn't only doing this for myself, but I was bringing truth to my family! I had a responsibility.

As my friend and I prepared for the podcast, we stayed in contact with the man who owned it to make sure things would go smoothly upon our arrival to his city. When I first saw this man, he reminded me of a guy I had known and dated, but after exchanging social media information, I noticed that he appeared extremely scary to me. I mentioned it to my friend, and I kept telling her about it but eventually, I let it go.

We were both excited for this opportunity and it was so refreshing to go to another city, just the both of us, to spread the Gospel and share our passions and purposes behind our business and to network.

One day, he randomly messaged me to check in to see how I was doing in preparation for the podcast. He was a stocky, tall man who looked like God was still delivering him from some things. I received his message and answered back without hesitation.

"I'm doing fine! Thanks again for this opportunity and for allowing my sis and me to share this platform with you in your city. We are greatly blessed," I said to him.

 He responded saying "no problem" and he couldn't wait for us to come and prepare for the podcast. To my understanding, the conversation had ended right then and there.

Hours later, he sent me another message asking if he could tell me something. I answered "sure."

He told me that he had feelings.

"For my friend?" I asked him immediately.

I asked that because he was so much older than me, just like my friend was and it would make sense that he would like her, but he said "no."

He had a crush on me.

I was shocked and confused at the same time, but I received it as a compliment and quickly ended the conversation.

As I had gotten older, I stopped liking or seeing myself with older men. Anything above five years older than me, I considered older. In this case, this man was 14 years older than me. Absolutely not! And again, for some reason, he really did look scary.

Although society had started to become extremely open and aware of some of the things that meant a lot to me and had started to expose, disrupt and dismantle the stigma of misogyny, patriarchy, trauma, sexism, pedophilia, and male biases, for me, it was still difficult to have these conversations honestly with my male peers, let alone an older man. Most of the time, older men were the ones who were more oblivious to these systems because it was their cultural norm at one point in time. They didn't want to let those mindsets, systems, and structures go, even when they were so-called "men of God."

I mentioned this to my friend and further explained that I was honestly not attracted to him, nor did I see myself with this man. I told her that I truly felt like this man would seriously hurt me and that for some reason, he scared me.

After that, I thought nothing more about it nor talked to him again before our scheduled podcast, which I continued to prepare myself for. All communication happened directly with my friend or in the group chat between all three of us.

Our travel day came.

My friend and I hurried to hit the road early in the morning to avoid hitting traffic and to get to his city in time. We were extremely excited! By this time, my friend and I had done many events together. Our business was our way of testifying of what God had done in our lives and how He had turned our mess into messages, and our breakthroughs into businesses. We were ready for God to use us on this platform!

We arrived at the studio right on time and hurried in to get settled since we were going live. Everything seemed okay between the man and me. There didn't seem to be any awkwardness.

As we started the podcast, we all got more comfortable and got deep into our dialogue. We thought the conversation was going to be about our businesses and stories, but it ended up being more about our perspectives on topics that our live audience asked. Nonetheless, we enjoyed it.

The man whose podcast we were on claimed that he was a believer like us and on the podcast, he stated that he always did a thing with his guests where he would tell them what he saw concerning them in the spirit.
 He looked at me and said "you remind me of Ruth. You're a hard worker who's focused."
 He then followed up, saying that he saw me as Ruth because I would soon be married, and my husband was coming as I continued to work.

I was a little skeptical, but I received it.

He did the same thing to my friend but with a whole different message.

We continued the conversation and finished the podcast.

We didn't even notice that we were done recording because we were so deep in dialogue on other matters. We began to talk about the church and the brokenness in it and what needs to change. He continued talking, admitting that his pain from the church was the reason he was where he was.

So moved by his transparency, I began to empathize with him and to see him in a different light. My friend and I asked him if it was alright if we prayed for him and he accepted. The glory of the Lord was so strong in the room that I began to cry because I felt for him. My heart warmed up to him and I started to feel bad for how I had responded to him when he messaged me.

Afterward, we left the studio, and my friend and I went back to our hotel.

I later messaged him to thank and bless him for letting us be on his podcast.

He responded immediately with four things:

"You guys did great, thanks for coming."

"Thank you for praying for me."
"I'm crushing on you, bad."
"What are you doing tonight?"

My friend and I were leaving the next day so that night was our last night in his city.

I was open to hanging out and getting to know him a little, so I didn't mind stepping out with him for a few hours.

I told my friend where I was going and that I would send her my location in case anything happened. She responded by telling me that she didn't think it was a good idea for me to go but I went anyway.

He asked me to come to him, so I drove to the address he provided and pulled up to his house.

He opened the door and let me in. It seemed very clean and nice. He then showed me around his house, and we eventually sat down at his desk and talked. He talked for hours, as I just listened to him and observed.

Something was off. I just didn't know what.

He started to pull out weed and then proceeded to roll up. He asked if I smoked, and I said "no."

I started talking a little and he just stared at me, licking his lips and expressing how much he was attracted to me. I started to also notice that he didn't care what I was saying at all. He seemed to only have one thing in mind.

He then looked at me and said that he saw me as a wife; "a good little Christian woman," he said. At that moment nothing else mattered. It was like I was finally here.

"Has my husband finally found me?" I thought to myself.

"It must be him. He saw me, and he approached me. It had to be! Right, God?"

After naming all the characteristics he saw in me, he followed up with, "but you know you have to submit, right?"

I nodded and said "yes."

"Okay, cool." He responded.

I felt so happy! Finally! After all the pain, tears, and prayers! My husband was here! He had found me. My heart was doing backflips inside my chest.

"Can I hold you?" He asked, disrupting my fantasy.

So blinded by my own fantasy, I eagerly responded "yes!"

He then turned the lights off, turned his music up on his speaker, and led me to his bedroom. It was at that moment that an alarm went off in my head. Sirens began going off all inside me and I got uncomfortable. He laid down on the bed while I stood and looked at him.

I thought to myself, "holding me doesn't require the bedroom."

"Come lay with me," he said.

As I walked towards the bed to get on, he grabbed me and started aggressively kissing me everywhere. I had no time to even breathe or completely touch the bed before he began to touch me. He turned me around and laid me on my back while pulling his pants down.

He then whispered in my ear, "let me make you my wife for the night."

"Let me fuck you."

"Let's fuck."

All the while, he was on top of me with his pants down.

My body went into full shock, and I couldn't move nor talk. I didn't want to have sex. I was hoping that he would get off me if I didn't respond, but no, he got even more aggressive.

He repeatedly said "say yes! You have to say yes! I'm not gonna force you. You have to say yes!" While he was yet forcing me.

My body was in full shock for about 10 minutes while he did and repeated the same thing. I realized that he wasn't going to move. So I slowly nodded my head up and down to say "yes."

At that moment, my mind went into survival mode, and I engaged so I could make it through the night.

I didn't know what to call what had just happened to me, so I called it sex. I lied about what had happened when I talked to the people close to me because I wasn't ready to face the reality of it and I felt that it was my fault, so I decided I was going to fix it myself.

A few weeks away from the baptism and I was starting to slowly drift away from God. I didn't acknowledge it or care because I was so stressed out trying to fix my situation.

Again, I wasn't ready to be vulnerable and I noticed once again that I was trying to justify and protect my abuser.

If people knew what had happened, they would make me feel like it was my fault. But I was already feeling that way.

Once again, I was that little girl on the side of my house being assaulted. I was so afraid of how people would respond. I also wasn't ready for everyone else's emotions because I hadn't yet faced my own.

My mind was in a constant survival mode that was later identified as "Stockholm syndrome."

I tried to form a romantic relationship with him and chose to believe he was my husband and that he was going to marry me. I thought about all the nice things he had said to me so I could continue to feed the fantasy I had created and deny the truth.

"Maybe, it really was just sex!"

"It's me! I engaged in this and it's okay because he's my husband," I tried telling myself.

After trying to make all the excuses, I had visions of that night every day and I knew something was wrong. I just didn't know what.

I decided that I would go back to his city after my baptism.

I felt obligated to try and date him so I could fix this, but I needed to change the narrative that it was my fault.

July 3rd came, and the next day was the scheduled day for me to get baptized.

I messaged the church secretary and told her that I wanted to reschedule!

"I'm not going to get baptized. I'm not clean," I thought to myself.

I was going to go back to his city the following week to do God knows what so I couldn't get baptized!

July 4th came quicker than I expected. I sang on the praise team that Sunday but there was such a heavyweight on me. The Holy Spirit was moving so much that I felt like I couldn't escape the move of God.

My Pastor was preaching about that day being Independence Day since it was the Fourth of July, but he was declaring spiritual freedom on everyone in the congregation. He preached that the bondage of sin was what most of us had been a slave to. I felt so guilty and heavy that I couldn't help but change my mind. I needed to get freedom that day! I needed to be free.

I rushed to the church secretary in the middle of service and told her that I was still getting baptized. She smiled at me and told me to go downstairs to get out of my "grave clothes."

I went downstairs to prepare and heard my friend praying, asking God to "trouble the water."

I was confused.

"Trouble the water? Like the song the slaves used to sing?"

But it hit me in the spirit. "Trouble the water" comes from the story of the blind man in the Bible by the Siloam pool. People with physical challenges and problems stood by the pool waiting for the angel of the Lord to stir it up, or in other words, to trouble the water. When the water was troubled, the first sick person who would step in would be healed.

I needed God to do that for me! So I started praying too!

"God trouble the water for me!"

Even though I had overcome so much in my life, was walking in my purpose, and was getting closer to God, I started to feel distant from God and myself in ways I didn't understand. I felt like I kept going through the same cycles. Though I had healed and though I had done so much work, things still weren't turning around for me. I thought I should have been, but I was not okay.

So maybe, just maybe this water would do something for me.

Just like in the Bible, the four of us who were getting baptized that day stood in line next to the pool of water. One by one, we were all cleansed and came back up with the Holy Ghost, speaking in tongues of fire!

How is it that I had experienced such a powerful move and had many things shift in me that day, yet I still felt the duty to save this situation with this man?

He barely talked to me after our first trip. I was the one who always reached out to him and when I did, most of the conversation was about sex. I didn't pay attention to that though; I just wanted to fix what had happened by getting in a relationship with him.

I left for his city 3 weeks after my baptism and when I got there that Friday, it was like more red flags began to appear from left to right. It became clear as day that he wasn't who I tried to make him out to be.

First, I drove to him, running off my own money and gas. Consideration should have told him to ask if I needed help financially but that wasn't the case. There was no kind of hospitality when I got there. He didn't offer me any food or care. In fact, I went to the store and bought groceries to put in his house. His house that had been neat and clean the first time was now dirty and disgusting.

He complained every day about how broke he was. He made it clear to me that he didn't want a relationship or marriage, but he didn't mind if we linked up and had sex when we were in each other's city. He kept saying and emphasizing that he was single, but I wasn't and kept boasting about how women were all over him. He would leave for "work" and leave me cooped up alone in the house.

On one of the days I was staying with him, he texted me that he was on his way home from work. Two minutes later, I heard a knock on his door. I thought that it was the next-door neighbor, so I thought nothing of it. The person knocked three more times, so I went to the door, and it was him.

He walked through the house, furious, asking, "where is he?!"

"Who?" I answered, scared and confused.

"You have someone in this house, don't you!! You had someone over this house when I wasn't here!" He yelled.

I looked at him and responded calmly, "you've got to be fucking kidding me."

He apologized immediately and blamed it on the devil.

"It's the devil making me think these things. You must be understanding when I respond this way."

I chose to overlook it and move on because I understood that he was traumatized by something from his past.

He had many other outbursts like these where he would turn aggressive and paranoid out of nowhere. Anytime I left the house, he would tell me to hurry and come back so no one would talk to me. His toxic and problematic responses didn't change at all. He decided to cut me off and block me the following week because he said I was ruining his life. From the first physical encounter with him to when I came back to his city, he never used a condom.

I was so stressed, and my body started responding in ways that were different to me, so I started thinking that I was possibly pregnant.

When I told him that there was a possibility that I was pregnant, he cussed me out every day until I found out that I wasn't. He would tell me that "he hated talking to me. He hated me. I needed to abort. I shouldn't want to be pregnant. I had messed up his life. He wasn't giving up his life for me and that he wouldn't be in the child's life."

Maybe him leaving me was God's hand over me like with the Shapeshifter. Maybe it was a blessing.

"But how is it that I am supposed to feel free, but I am burdened all over again? I am now more burdened than I have ever been before.

"Shattered
Empty
Broken

Shattered
Torn
Confused

How did I let you do this to me?
Somewhere along the way
I lost who I used to be.

Angry
Frustrated
Confused

Lonely
Depressed
Misused

I didn't know this is how marriage is supposed to be
No one ever said that this would be easy.

I'm giving this to you, Lord.

I can't do this anymore

I gave my heart and he walked right out that door.

Shattered
Broken
Confused

Shattered
Torn
Misused"

THE REMNANT

I hated myself. I hated every ounce of my existence. I couldn't get around the fact that it was my fault! I was, once again, willing to sacrifice my dignity, worth, and self-respect for a ring he was never going to give me.

"Did I heal? Did I even grow? How did this happen again?"

Again, I ignored the signs. The only solution left was to die.

Even though I had already tried to commit suicide before, I had never felt like my soul was dead like it did right then. I had never felt that way before.

"Why did I lie again?"

I had never felt my soul lament so deeply before.

I remembered watching the movie Women of Brewster Place as a girl. I remembered watching the scene where Ciel was lying in her bed, looking dead on the inside but on the outside still breathing. She had lost everything and didn't know how to keep going. The only reason she survived was because she had Mrs. Mattie, who came in every day to fight for her when she couldn't fight for herself until she finally could.

The only difference between Ciel and I was instead of Mrs. Mattie, I had the whispers of God in my ear reminding me of the promises He had for me. God promised me that He would restore everything that the swarming locusts stole from me. He told me that I had work to do. He told me that I would speak for those who couldn't speak for themselves. He told me that He had so much for me to do. He promised me that He had someone for me.

God reminded me that I had come too far to not get my reward. Even though I wanted to die, I had to choose to live again. Despite the moments when I didn't want to wake up at all, I had to choose to live again. Although I had to try to heal while in tears, I had to choose to live again. Despite the lies whispered by the enemy, I had to choose to live again. Despite people not believing me, I had to choose to live again. Despite what people may say, I had to choose to live again. Despite people not understanding why I would lie, I had to choose to live again. Despite people turning their backs on me in the process, I had to choose to live again.

This would not be the end of my story. The hope that I had of seeing the promises God fulfilled in my life was my remnant.

"I know
that you left me here to die
But through it all
I will survive
I know
I'm gonna make it
I've gotta make it
Cause I know you're still God
And you'll see me through this."
Tamar Davis

"So take it all away
Take it all away
'Til all that's left is You
Take it all away, take it all
Take it all away take it all
Take it all away
'Til all that's left is You"
-    Maverick City Music

UNLEARNING, RELEARNING AND ESTHER

I hated God.

I was back at square one.

I felt like all the work I had done was undone.

I felt like it didn't matter.

All the books I had read, all the therapy sessions, and all the mentoring sessions had been pointless.

They had all meant nothing.

I had hated God before, but I had always had faith.

This time I was losing faith. I couldn't see God anymore. This was the first time in my life that I felt empty.

I was over it. I was tired of this healing process. I was tired of the failed relationships. I was tired of not seeing the promises come to pass.

I felt scammed by God.

The niggas I ran into were all fucking trash.

Now, I had to not only heal from this situation but I also had to do something different so I wouldn't respond to trauma like this anymore.

Sometime had gone by and it was my second follow-up with my new therapist since we reconnected. I had started seeing her a year prior. I had continued to keep a therapist in my corner since college. She was a black woman so therapy with her was extremely different from all my other counselors and therapists. She held me accountable, and she was black like me. Most days I hated it, but I needed every minute of it.

"Why do I continue to keep getting myself in the same situation? I trusted someone again, avoided seeing the truth and he left me. He was so narcissistic and verbally abusive," I expressed to my therapist.

She listened to me vent then started asking me questions. She had noticed that I was saying a lot of things that I hadn't said in my last session.

I vented most of our session about how horrible this man was. I confessed that I had noticed patterns and bad behaviors in the beginning but again I had wanted to believe what I wanted to believe.

"What happened in the beginning? You didn't say any of this in our last session." She stated that she would have never encouraged certain things between this man and me if she would have known all that I was expressing to her now.

When we had our first session after reconnecting, I had painted a picture of this man to make him seem like a whole different person. She wasn't the only one. There were many others I lied to about what had happened between him and me. But just like Scripture says, "beware of false prophets, who come to you in sheep's clothing, but inwardly they are ravenous wolves. You will know them by their fruits. Do men gather grapes from thornbushes or figs from thistles?" Matthew 7:15-16

As I started to unpack everything from the day, I met this man in person to when he blocked me, I realized that the speculations I had prior to even meeting him were my spiritual discernment.

Why did I ignore it, is the question, and most importantly, why did I lie?

This wasn't my first rodeo in responding this way and that is why it hurt me so much. I thought I was past it. I thought I would never experience it again. I had healed!

"Most people who have been abused before, respond the way that you did. You have been abused before, so it is common," my therapist said to confirm what I was already thinking.

"Did you even tell him yes when he was on top of you?" She asked.

"No," I responded. "But I knew that this would happen! God showed me signs!" I said beating myself up.

"Why is it so hard for you to believe who people are when they show you the first time?"

Feeling ashamed, I answered the question to the best of my ability.

"I'm a believer, and I am the evidence that God changes people. I have witnessed and seen that people can change."

"But that's not up to you to decide if they want to change or not or even when or how. You must accept the reality of people. People will show you who they are if you let time reveal it to you by just watching and listening."

She told me that what had happened wasn't my fault. I couldn't have done anything to change him or the situation.

The truth is I was embarrassed. Again, I wasn't as strong as I portrayed myself to be. Ending up responding to situations like this made me feel sad for myself. I had been through so much and had never told anyone.

I had tried to tell my story to people before but I would either end up damaged or unheard because people were uneducated and lacked compassion. I learned to just go on in life and not tell anyone the parts that I hid deep inside because I didn't want to get cut again by broken people.

In that, I learned not to trust anyone with the sensitive parts of me which is why I lied about being raped. I couldn't fathom someone responding to me the same way people did when I was sexually assaulted and physically abused. I got so used to lying and covering up whenever I experienced a threatening situation

My therapist told me that I now had to do the hard part.

I was confused because I felt like I did everything I was supposed to do. What else do I possibly need to do?

"Unlearn," she responded.

I had gone through the same cycles without realizing it. Though I had been single for almost 3 years, I was still doing the same thing.

I chose the same type of guys.

I got with the Counterfeit, a man with a form of Godliness but no fruit. I got my hopes up because he had the potential. Then I got heartbroken because he turned out to be someone different when in reality, he was always that way. He just knew how to dress it up well.

I got with the Placeholders because they would help me feel the void from the heartbreak I experienced with the Counterfeit.

Then I would get abused by Shapeshifters or Predators and feel like it was my fault.

And it was all because even when I knew something wasn't going to work, I still wanted it to force it to work and when I got abused, I would still respond like that broken little girl and try to fix it. My response was to fix the situation to gain some kind of control over a problem that was completely outside my control.

Feeling out of control is what I had hated the most as a little girl so feeling out of control reminded me of myself as that helpless little girl. It broke me. It scared me and would result in me responding out of trauma.

Most of the relationships I had been in were trauma bonds and soul ties. I didn't know how to get any other type of man.

I knew that I should have never stayed in those relationships, but I did because I wanted to fix them. I felt like successful relationships meant I was worthy and valuable so when relationships didn't work, I would start seeing myself negatively. I didn't feel valuable or worthy anymore because none of my relationships had worked out.

Then I would try to turn situations where I was abused into normal situations because I was so traumatized. I hated being viewed as broken or weak so I thought normalizing my abusive experiences and trying to fix them by staying in those relationships would maybe change the narrative of what was happening or what had already happened.

Prior to my therapist telling me to unlearn, I hadn't realized that my family's inability to deal with their own emotions and leaving their trauma unprocessed, so they could try to live as normal a life as possible, was teaching me to do the same.

I was never taught to identify my emotions, process them or deal with them. I was taught to be strong and to be strong was to endure as much pain, trauma, hardship, and heartbreak as possible and still show up, even if I was dying inside or was already dead. In other words, be emotionally absent or unavailable.

No one taught me that to feel was okay or that feeling itself is not a good or bad thing. It just is.

No one taught me that feelings were supposed to be felt. Sad, mad, happy, embarrassed, to feel it all to the highest capacity, and then when my heart was ready to let go of that feeling, I let it go. I never learned any of that.

So I grew up trying to deny the purest, most natural parts of me, shoving feelings and experiences away because I didn't know what to do with them and then blowing up and exploding when I couldn't contain and hold it in anymore.

I didn't know then that when I tried to shove emotions down and deny them, they came out in my behavior and in everything I did. Because I was an expressive person who felt things fully, I learned to self-sabotage by suppressing what I felt and what I went through, making me numb to life at a very young age.

I didn't look for love. I looked for relief.

I allowed myself to be in situations that I knew weren't good for me. I learned how to believe false realities and fantasize about things that were fake. I would get mad when things didn't turn out the way I wanted them to and then blame God.

So to feel something other than the pain, I became addicted to codependent relationships and sex to distract myself and when I couldn't have those two things, I would be forced to cry out to God.

God needed me to get to the end of myself. He needed me to get to the end of my dysfunction, codependency, and addictions so He could put me back together. I needed to get to the end where I could pay for my sins. I deserved death.

I sat in His face and chose my way. My way led me to death! But the debt was already paid.

I believe God already knew that His people would go through situations like these, so He understood. That was the point of Jesus dying on the cross and being slain as the ultimate sacrifice.

I believe God understood why I did what I did. I didn't know any better and I had to offer grace to myself because of that.

"I'm broken. I'm sinful and wicked! But God saw fit to rescue me."

This unhealthy way of coping was what I had been subconsciously taught though. Some things I learned on my own because I wasn't taught anything else.

Though my family should be responsible for how I ended up, the decisions I made and what I had gone through were on me. I couldn't blame them.

I couldn't blame my mother for not knowing how to choose the right partners in relationships.

I couldn't blame my mother for not teaching me how to protect and handle having a big heart like herself.

I couldn't blame my mother for not being able to teach me how not to fix men and situations that I had no control over.

I couldn't blame my mother for not going to therapy and not getting the help she needed mentally and emotionally because, during that time, those resources were not popular or in reach for her as a black woman.

My mother did the best she could with what she had and what she knew.

Same with my father, I couldn't blame him for not being there because my grandfather wasn't in his life growing up either.

He did the best he could with what he had.

Neither one of them could teach us, equip us or protect us.

They didn't have the resources, education, and support like my generation does today and for that, I forgave them.

I don't hate them for doing whatever they had to do to survive, for themselves and for us.

I also realized that my parents didn't have the best teachers to be educated emotionally or be mentally aware. They didn't know because no one taught them.

I chose to believe that if my parents, grandparents, great grandparents, and the people before them knew better, they would have done better, not only for us but for themselves as well.

I forgave them.

"But the time is now for it to end with me.

I now must get out of agreement with that way of thinking and lifestyle because the time is now.

I am now out of agreement with survival mentally. I will now live.

I am now out of agreement with responding from a place of trauma. I have support around me, and it is safe enough to not hide or lie anymore.

I am now out of agreement with trauma bonding. I am now only receiving and accepting relationships that are divine and ordained.

I am now out of agreement with places and people who still agree and live in things I am out of agreement with.

I am now out of agreement with the intrusive thoughts that make me believe fake realities that make me continue to live in fear and hopelessness."

During that time of unlearning, I realized that what I was doing was overcoming. My therapist told me in one session that it was now my duty to tell my story. Me telling my story was helping me heal, unlearn, and be set free.

I also learned to come out of agreement with trauma bonding. In order to come out of agreement with my trauma-bonding with men, I had to come out of agreement with the WAY I trauma bonded which was in my need to protect. I connected with broken little boys because I was still a broken little girl. I wanted to protect them. I protected my Shapeshifter's broken little boy hoping he would turn around and do the same for me. I was so fearful and traumatized of my reputation being tarnished by the Shapeshifter that I didn't notice and continued trying to protect others. Just like my issue with abandonment, I was unable to leave men because I knew how it felt to be left.

"But now, I'm not that broken little girl who was abandoned. The scarlet letter on my chest stands for "Atoned" now, and I come out of agreement not only with abandonment and everything attached to it but also with protecting the reputations of those who have hurt me. I get to tell my side of the story now with no guilt, shame, or trauma attached to it."

Along with telling my side of the story came the realization that I would need to stop telling my story like I was on trial. A friend of mine, during this time of unlearning, noticed that every time I was telling my side of a story, I would tell it like I was trying to prove to the person I was talking to that what happened to me was true. She told me, "Kayla, you are not guilty!"

"Kayla, you are not guilty."

She told me to rest in that. I had been telling my story as if I was on trial when I wasn't. It was sad to realize that I had been through so much that I felt like I had to do that.

I had to be free with no restraints. This was my experience, and I was not on trial!

We overcome by two things: the blood of the Lamb and the word of our testimony according to Revelations 12:11

My therapist told me that she was going to hold me accountable to tell my story...the whole story.

I was comfortable with certain parts of my story but not all of it. It was because when I would tell it, it wouldn't be in safe spaces, and I would end up wounded more than before.

My therapist told me that it didn't matter what people said or what they did. It didn't change the narrative of my story or change the fact that it needed to be told.

Even though the unlearning process was needed, so was Jesus.

"So if the son sets you free, you will be free indeed." John 8:36

I needed to heal so I could identify what I needed to pray about, come out of agreement with and unlearn.

I had to believe that there was power in telling our story.

I thought to myself, "but what if I get talked about?"

"What if they say I lied?"

"What about the people who have told their stories and died because of it? People have died for telling their stories! What if I die?" I said fearfully.

But then I was reminded of Esther. Esther, in the Bible, was a nobody at one point and then became a Queen. Her King didn't know she was a Jew when he married her and made her Queen and then later decided to have the Jewish people annihilated.

When the time came for him to kill off the Jews, she had to decide to speak up and save her people or let them die.

Mordecai, her uncle, told her what if this was the very thing she was purposed to do? To save her people by getting access to the kingdom and being connected to the King the way she was.

Even in fear, she chose to be brave and fast and pray and then speak up.

She got to the point where she decided that no matter what happened, she was going to do what she felt purposed to do.

It was against the law for a woman to speak to a man unless she was spoken to, let alone summon a king without first being summoned and speak without permission.

Despite that, she was encouraged and coined the phrase "if I perish, I perish" meaning "if I I die, let me die but I'll do it for my people."

I immediately started to wonder, "how many people have stories just like me and never knew what to do with them?"

"How many people are silently dying because of this same fear that Esther and I had?"

I had to decide like Esther to be free, and help others be free, or be afraid and continue to let God's people die of trauma in their mental prisons.

And just like Esther, I chose to speak up and help save God's people.

"And if I perish, I perish."

Though I had done all this work of praying, unlearning, coming out of agreement with things, and healing, God showed me that I needed to come out of agreement with other things as well.

God spoke to me one day and said, "retrace your steps."

I replied, "huh?"

He told me again to retrace my steps.

God told me to go back to the place where I almost killed myself.

He told me I had to fall out of agreement with death by suicide.

I was so scared and intimidated by that.

"What if the same people who hurt me see me? What would they say? What would they do?"

Again, God said to go back.

I went back to my hometown, and I did just that.

I arrived at the church, to the place where the first group of people who were Christians hurt me and where I hurt me. I parked my car and stared at the church building. The song that was playing in my car was "Build My Life" by Maverick City Music and Trbl.

The Scripture that came up in my mind while I stood there with my eyes closed, was Psalms 23, starting at verse 4.

"Yea, though I walk through the valley of the shadow of death, I will fear no evil; For You are with me; Your rod and Your staff, they comfort me. You prepare a table before me in the presence of my enemies; You anoint my head with oil; My cup runs over. Surely goodness and mercy shall follow me All the days of my life, And I will dwell in the house of the Lord Forever."

I continued standing there with my eyes closed and started saying things like:

"You are free."

"Now it's time to live."

"I come out of agreement with death."

And suddenly God gave me a vision.

God showed me my car parked in the neighborhood where I had attempted to crash my it a few years back.

God showed me my car swarmed around by demons and angels, one group praying and the other preying.

God arrived and dismissed both groups and got in the car next to me as I was sleeping and said, "Talitha Koum" which means "little girl, I say to you, arise."

This was the same exact thing that happened in Mark 5:41 when the daughter of a Pharisee named Jaruis was pronounced dead. And though some were weeping, others saw Jaruis looking for Jesus to bring his daughter back to life and to save her and they tried to discourage him and tell him to let her go.

He got a hold of Jesus and when Jesus came, He dismissed everyone but the parents.

He looked at the little girl and said, "she is not dead, she is sleeping. Talitha Koum! Little girl, I say to you, arise."

God told me to forgive myself. God told me to forgive the broken me for hurting myself and doing whatever I needed to do to survive. He told me that forgiving that part of me would be the last part before I could be free.

I did.

I forgave me.
I forgave Kayla.

That was the last part for me to do. I wiped my tears, got into my car, and drove off.

But as I drove off, I looked at the church and whispered, "I forgive you too."

After releasing myself, I forgave the church, all the Shapeshifters, the Predator, and all the people who cut me along the way, in my journey.

"I forgive you."

I returned home that night and God spoke to me again.

"How is it that you reconcile and forgive everyone else but Me, your Father, the One who withheld things from you, the One you blamed and hated. Tell me how you feel. I can take it."

Surprised, I said "really?"

"Yes," he said.

"Okay," I responded and then I took a deep breath.

"I hated you. You allowed so much chaos and trauma into my life. You watched me suffer each time I was abused and abandoned. Why didn't you stop it? Why did I have to go through so much? When everyone else had a two-parent home, got married, and started their lives with the one they loved, I was home in tears over what had happened to me. Why did you give me the desire to be married anyway, if You were going to make me go through all of this? I feel like You lied to me. I feel like I was made a fool! You said in Your Word that your people would never be put to shame. But I felt like I was. I lost faith in you! That last promise was never fulfilled! You are a liar and I hate you. I should have never trusted you."

THE PROMISE PART 1

It felt like God had been silent this whole time until now.

He first directed me to a Scripture:

"And we know that all things work together for good to those who love God, to those who are called according to *His* purpose."
Romans 8:28

He said "I heard when you were a little girl and prayed for Me to take away your anger issue. I heard you but instead of removing it, I taught you how to control it and I turned you into a woman of God who became a warrior in the spirit. You've become a woman who speaks and walks with the fire of God inside of her. That little girl who was once afraid has been able to look death in the face on many occasions and speak my Word to it unapologetically. That little girl who was confused was humble enough to learn and now I have put you in different positions to teach my people what you have learned. That fatherless little girl got the advantage and benefits of experiencing Me at a young age, in a strong and peculiar way that many, with both parents, will never get to experience or will only experience much later in life."

He reminded me next of another Scripture: Deuteronomy 14:2

"For you *are* a holy people to the Lord your God, and the Lord has chosen you to be a people for Himself, a special treasure above all the peoples who *are* on the face of the earth."

God wasn't done.

"All of the tears you cried from being bullied because you were different and hating yourself turned you into a bold woman of God who walks in her full self with complete fearlessness and humility. A woman who now knows all where she has been and what she has gone through, finally found her identity in Christ and will be a vessel, lampstand, lighthouse, and bold witness for Me."

He led me back to the New Testament giving me a revelation of His grace.

John 8:36 "Therefore if the son makes you free, you shall be free indeed."

"Do you remember how you were a slave to sin and your connections with broken people almost killed you? I saved you from fornication and showed you how to live a holy and sanctified life. I cleaned you when you were in your own filth. You enjoyed your sinful nature, soul ties, and trauma. I still set you free when you didn't even see it as freedom. I elevated you and separated you from things and people who couldn't go where you were going. I set you free from those who wanted you dead and acted like they loved you. I not only set you free physically, but I set your mind free and made you unlearn the life of a sinner and made you whole!"

"You were like Mary Magdalene with 7 demons, the Samaritan woman who had multiple husbands and was outcasted by everyone in her village, the woman with the issue of blood who had an issue only I could heal, and the girl who was dead, all because you lacked faith and your sin was killing you. Just like them, I turned you all into the woman from Ezekiel 16:8"

"When I passed by you again and looked upon you, indeed your time *was* the time of love; so I spread My wing over you and covered your nakedness. Yes, I swore an oath to you and entered a covenant with you, and you became Mine," says the Lord God."

"I set you free. Can't you see?"

"Did you forget how I protected you? "He asked.

"No weapon formed against you shall prosper,
And every tongue *which* rises against you in judgment
You shall condemn.
This *is* the heritage of the servants of the Lord,
And their righteousness *is* from Me,"

Says the Lord" Isaiah 54:17

"I brought you so far and allowed you to heal! You didn't go backward."

"Do you remember how I gave you grace every time you trusted your sinful heart?" He asked me again.

"No temptation has overtaken you except as is common to man; but God *is* faithful, who will not allow you to be tempted beyond what you are able, but with the temptation will also make the way of escape, that you may be able to bear *it*." 1 Corinthians 10:13

"Did I ever leave you? When have you ever been alone?" He asked lastly.

"You wanted a life free from pain and suffering, daughter, there isn't one. I never said it would be easy. I told you that I was never going to leave you."

"I have protected you from every Goliath, thing, and person, seen and unseen. Every traumatic experience and through every mental challenge I have been with you. I have been with you through every panic attack, every flashback, every suicidal thought, and every attempt. I kept you. I fought for you. I gave you a way of escape every time even when you blamed Me for putting you there and hated Me for it. I took it all and loved you despite it all. I heard you every time you called My Name and came to rescue you from every situation you put yourself in. My army delivered you every time. There is nothing that should make you fear because I am with you always. Look at My record! The righteous never have and never will be forsaken. My people will never be put to shame. I wept every time you wept! Every time you cried; I was right there. I saved every tear!"

"I allowed you to feast on days you should have starved. I have always provided for you!"

"I have dealt with those people who abused you or I will deal with them on Judgement Day because I am a Just God. I am not pleased with what was done to you, daughter. But let me deal with them with my love. I turned it all around for you. I handled everything that was meant to kill you."

"Do you know how victorious you are?" He boldly asked.

"Jesus said to her, "Did I not say to you that if you would believe you would see the glory of God?" John 11:40

"When you let me finish the work I started: healing you, molding you, making you, delivering you, changing you, you will see My glory revealed in you. I did not forget the other things I promised you. I know what is best for you, and when it's best to give it to you. Trust me again. I did not fail you and never did. Let me finish My work in you and for you.

"I am your father!" He spoke.

"I will never withhold any good thing from you. I am a God of my Word! When you thought I wasn't answering your prayer and fulfilling the promise I made, I was preparing you to be the woman to obtain the promise and not destroy it when I gave it to you. I not only wanted you to heal but I needed you to become whole and I needed everything in you that destroyed, aborted, and miscarried the promise to be flushed out of you, unlearned, disconnected, divorced, and fallen out of agreement with. The promise is bigger than you! The promise is so much more than you are receiving a husband. It is more than a piece of paper, hanging out, having companionship, and feeling loved. You and your husband will be leaders and ambassadors for my Kingdom. You will both win souls individually and together. This will be an authentic covenant that will represent My love for the church. And when it's time, I the Lord will make it happen." (Isaiah 60:22)

My eyes began to swell in repentance. I did remember, I remembered it all. I not only acknowledged what He had done but I acknowledged what He was and is still doing now. I started remembering the things God had done for me and I couldn't help but exalt Him and give Him thanks.

God turned my mourning into dancing, my miserable days into beautiful days. He rescued me from every trap of the enemy and every trap I put myself in. He allowed me to be lifted and supported in seasons I thought I would never overcome. He allowed me to use every stone that was thrown at me, to build a platform to not only speak and preach to His people but to show the devil that God did not fail. God allowed me to see victory in more ways than one. No weapon formed against me, none of the traps that the enemy set out for me, or the schemes and devices he tried to use to destroy me, prospered. God covered, protected, and defended me. God showed me constantly that He would use every part of me in different seasons, circumstances, and situations.

"Kayla, you have arrived."

All I could say at that moment was "sorry."

I had allowed my impatience and the schemes of the Devil to create distance between God and me. I had allowed my anger towards God to create division and destruction between us. With that anger already being evident at the center of our relationship, it was easy for the devil to seep in and create more of a divide between us and destroy my faith and relationship with God completely.

"In your anger do not sin. Do not let the sun go down while you are still angry, and do not give the devil a foothold." Ephesians 4:26-27

This Scripture isn't just about me loving my neighbor but it's for my relationship with God as well. I can't let the Devil keep having a foothold in my relationship with God.

Now, when I have an issue with God, I'm going to go to Him first and not let the sun go down on my anger. The same standards I have in relationships with people are the same I'm going to have in my relationship with God. I can't lose Him and me again.

No, I am not saying I have arrived at a place free from trouble, pain, or trauma. Instead, I've arrived at a place where when trouble, trauma, and pain come my way, I can be like the Proverbs 31:21 woman.

"She is not afraid of snow for her household,

For all her household *is* clothed with scarlet."

- She is me
- Instead of being afraid, I will be brave even if I feel afraid when troubles come my way.
- Snow represents a season of cold, hardship, or things dying.
- Household is me and my temple (heart, soul) and actual home or safe places where I find peace.
- Scarlet is a red color and red represents the blood of Jesus

Let's rephrase the Scripture. "I will not be afraid when troubles come, yet I will be brave because I am covered by the blood from the inside out."

This is enough evidence for me to trust and believe God for whatever I don't see right now. This is enough evidence to trust that the rest of the promise will come in His timing and in God's way. I trust that God knows what is best for me and when.

"The least of you will become a thousand,

the smallest, a mighty nation.

I am the Lord.

in time I will do this swiftly." Isaiah 60:22

The reality is things will happen and I will be angry with God again and times will get hard again. But instead of letting my circumstances take me backward, I will pick up my rod, which represents the power of the Blood, and remember the testimonies of how God never failed me. I will pick up my staff which represents my tools such as my support system and the strategies I had learned in the process of becoming whole.

"And they overcame him by the blood of the Lamb and by the word of their testimony, and they did not love their lives to the death." Revelations 12:11

There isn't a better time than now to overcome and choose to continuously overcome regardless of our circumstances. The time isn't now for me alone but now for you as well.

I am now inviting you into this process with these truths:

The time is now to be brave.

The time is now to overcome.

The time is now to get the help and support you need.

The time is now to overcome.

The time is now to walk in the totality of your purpose.

The time is now to overcome.

The time is now to stop being ashamed.

The time is now to overcome.

The time is now to release.

The time is now to overcome.

The time is now to trust again.

The time is now to overcome.

The time is now to run back to Jesus.

The time is now to overcome.

The time is now to heal.

The time is now to overcome.

The time is now to get back everything the Devil stole.

The time is now to overcome.

The time is now to let your gifts make room for you.

The time is now to overcome.

The time is now to embrace the black sheep you are.

The time is now to overcome.

The time is now to be unmovable when the storms come.

The time is now to overcome.

The time is now to be more of a testimony than a test.

The time is now to overcome.

The time is now to make room for more.

The time is now to overcome.

The time is now to try again.

The time is now to overcome.

The time is now to break out of these cycles.

The time is now to overcome.

The time is now to be disciplined and healthy.

The time is now to overcome.

The time is now to be holy.

The time is now to overcome.

The time is now for chains to break.

The time is now to overcome.

The time is now for strongholds to be brought down.

The time is now to overcome.

The time is now to live.

The time is now to overcome.

The time is now to unlearn.

The time is now to overcome.

The time is now to relearn.

The time is now to overcome.

The time is now to shift your mindset from just living to being alive.

The time is now to overcome.

The time is now to go from victim to victorious.

The time is now to overcome.

The time is now to let go of the survival mindset.

The time is now to overcome.

The time is now to close the door to that season.

The time is now to overcome.

The time is now to walk in victory.

The time is now to overcome.

The time is now to experience true love.

The time is now to overcome.

The time is now to be redeemed by God for His perfect will.

The time is now to overcome.

"Kayla, how do I allow myself to be redeemed for God's perfect will?"

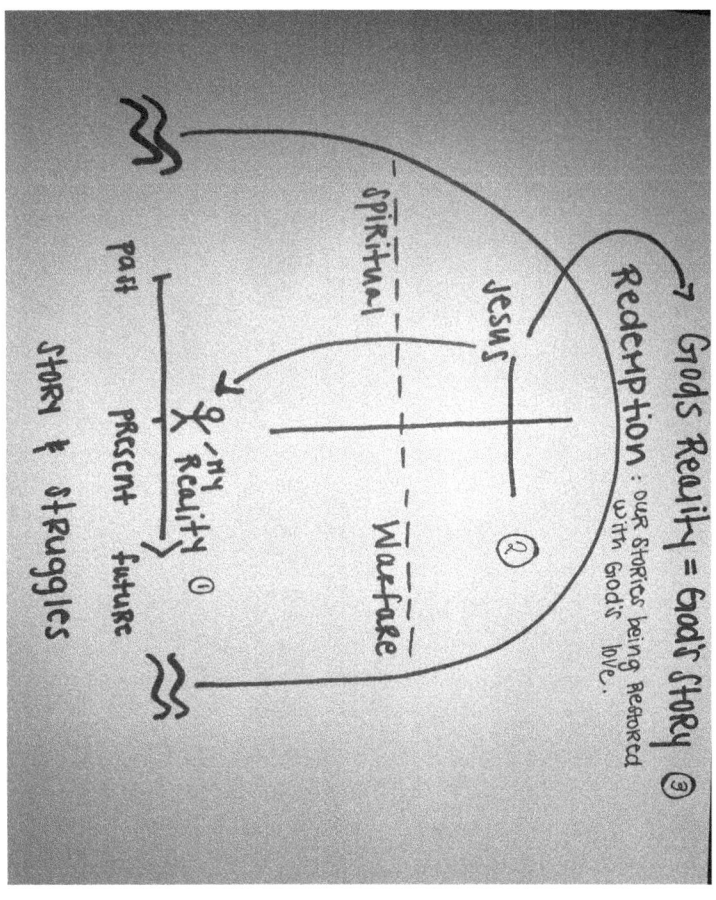

Above is an illustration I was taught. We have an arch that separates our earthly experiences from God and the heavens. What we experience on earth will be a combination of suffering, achievements, victories, and pains from when we are children all the way to when God sees fit to take us to Heaven. On earth, we can experience Jesus. Whenever we allow Him to be our Savior, He redeems us and changes our story. We go from being an orphan to being sons and daughters in Jesus. Jesus is the only way to God the Father. In the illustration, at the top, it states God's Reality- God's way to get us there is through His redemption. We must submit our lives to God. It is not about us, but about God! He is the main character, and we are the prompts being used to show the ultimate love story.

Under the arch, on the earth, we will experience troubles, detours, setbacks, and schemes from the enemy to steal our focus and time, kill the will God has for our life and destroy our faith so we don't fulfill the purpose. We were created to be loved but because of sin, we experience pain and trauma. Nonetheless, God had a specific plan for you and your life even before you were in your mother's womb. You had a purpose then and you have that same purpose now and in order to be used for God's perfect will, we must fully come out of agreement with our wants, desires, and our wills and agree with God's will and give Him full control. Yes, full control, because the time is now.

Now you have witnessed God allowing me to overcome, accept myself fully and walk completely in my person.

Do you realize what I did?

I testified.

In Hebrew, the word testimony is translated to "Aydooth". Aydooth means 'repeat or do it again.' The same way God restored me and is still restoring me is the same way He will do it for you. God will do it again for you. God will repeat it for you, and when He does it for you, you will tell another, and tell another and soon, we will all sing the same song telling the world that God had finished what He started; that God redeems; that the blood still works and that the name of Jesus never lost its power. It's not the end. It's the beginning of your journey. The time is now.

"And I'll testify of the battles You've won
How You were my portion when there
wasn't enough

And I'll testify of the seas that we've
crossed

The waters You parted, the waves that I've
walked

Singing, oh-oh-oh, my God did not fail

Oh-oh-oh, it's the story I'll tell

Singing, oh-oh-oh, I know it is well

Oh-oh-oh, it's the story I'll tell

And all that is left is highest praises, yeah,
yeah

So sing hallelujah to the Rock of Ages

Come on, sing it, all that's left

All that is left is highest praises, so sing it,
sing it

So sing hallelujah to the Rock, to the Rock
of Ages "

Acknowledgments

I want to acknowledge two people whose words and strategies influenced my healing and transformation the most and I talk about it in the book. I speak on a book called Longing for Daddy by Monique Robinson and the diagram I display at the end of the book that I was taught by Karen Cheong.

Karen Cheong was my Christian counselor for a season of my life and her and her husband's ministry "Restore" that I also went through and completed impacted my healing so much that I had to display the diagram that was taught to me. Their ministry was the first ministry that I ever saw and went through that displayed the marrying of two Jesus and therapy so ideal to me. This ministry helped renew my mind and perspective in my journey of brokenness to newness.

Although I have never met Monique Robinson and did not walk with her closely as Karen, her book alone had impacted me just as much.

I must formally thank them both for being obedient to writing their books and walking into their ministries which brought forth deliverance and healing in my life. In my book I do not take on their revelations and words as my own but instead I explain in the book how both in their work impact me and my journey with Jesus. My heart is full of gratitude because of them both and where I am now due to their influence on my life and overcoming process and would not be who I am today and where I am today without them. Again, thank you.

Songs Appendix

Page 26- Kirk Franklin. "Brighter Day"

Page 26- Marvin Sapp. "Never Would Have Made It"

Page 7- Maverick City Music. "Take Me Back"

Page 10- The Stylistics. "Stop, Look, List (To Your Heart)"

Page 11- The William Brothers. "I'm Just a Nobody"

Page 27- New Birth Total Praise Choir. "A New Beginning"

Page 29- BOYZ II Men. "Stand"

Page 36- Fred Hammond. "Lord, We Need Your Love"

Page 109& 112- Tamar Davis. "Shattered"

Page 138- Maverick City Music. "The Story I'll Tell"

Book Recommendations

Longing for Daddy: Healing from the Pain of an
Absent or Emotionally Distant Father
                              Book by Monique Robinson
Lost Letters to My Father
                              Book By Kevin Adams
Missing Mom Pieces
                              Book By Christy Lawyer